The Busy Girl's Guide to

cake
decorating

The Busy Girl's Guide to

cake decorating

Ruth Clemens

David and Charles

Contents

Introduction

Welcome to *The Busy Girl's Guide to Cake Decorating*! I'm guessing you have this book because you fancy your hand at a spot of cake decorating, you don't have much time and are the typical 'busy girl'. Well, you're in the right place. This book is all about cake decorating without the fuss, the palaver and sometimes the tears too!

The projects within the book are split into three sections. The **Evening Whip-Ups** (one-hour projects) are perfect when you have very little time, and are easy to throw together one evening after work. The **Half-Day Delights** (two-hour projects) are for when you have an afternoon to spare. Finally, the **Weekend Wonders** (three- to four-hour projects) are for when you've got a bit more time available in your schedule!

In cake-decorating terms, all of the above are tiny amounts of time – large, intricate projects take professional cake decorator's days, if not weeks, of work. We busy girls don't have the time or the patience (OK then, that's just me) to create those kinds of works of art but this book contains stunning projects that can be achieved in next to no time.

I cheat, I do things the quick way for maximum impact, I'll have 'traditional' cake decorators up in arms with my kamikaze ways but, hey, it is what it is and I was never one to toe the line. I am the typical busy girl (perhaps more the busy than the girl these days) – I have three young boys needing my attention, wanting punctures fixed, the paddling pool filling up and feeding every two minutes; a bustling household filled with family, friends and pets; and not forgetting the other 'boy' in the house, my husband. So here it is, *The Busy Girl's Guide to Cake Decorating* – the perfect place to start your foray into the world of cakes.

So let's get this show on the road – cake decorating – the busy girls' way…

Ruth

Get Ready

Equipment and ingredients
to help you prepare…

Equipment

Cake-decorating equipment can be expensive and specialist, however the projects in this book make the most of everyday items that you will find in any kitchen, supplemented with a few key pieces.

Essential items: baking

Food mixer

Sieve

Spoons and spatulas

Mixing bowls

Scales

Selection of cake tins (pans), baking trays, cupcake trays

Selection of cookie cutters

Measuring spoons

Greaseproof (wax) paper

Cupcake cases

Palette knife

Rolling pin

Ice cream scoop

Wire cooling rack

Essential items: decorating

Selection of small decorative cutters – blossoms, butterflies, stars, hearts etc.

Disposable piping (pastry) bags and selection of nozzles (tips)

Ribbons

Cake boards and cards

Serrated knife

Set of round cutters – straight-edged and fluted

Pearl-headed pins

Icing (confectioners') sugar shaker

Double-sided tape

Cocktail sticks (toothpicks)

Long sugarpaste (rolled fondant) rolling pin

Sharp knife

Edible gel paste colours

Icing smoother

Pastry brush and variety of paintbrushes

Edible lustre dusts

Coloured florists' wire

Dowels

Plastic egg tray or paint palette

Useful items

Posy picks

Pastry roller

Pizza cutter

Edible glue

Decorative buttons (for embossing)

Water spray/ mister

Serrated steak knife

Non-stick mat

Small sugarpaste (rolled fondant) rolling pin

Sugar sprinkles/ decorations – stars, coloured strands, pearls, silver heart and ball dragees etc.

Icing (confectioners') sugar duster (see opposite)

Make your own sugar duster

You will need a brand new all-purpose cleaning cloth, an elastic band and icing (confectioners') sugar. Lay the cloth open on your work surface and place two heaped tablespoons of sugar in the centre. Gather the cloth around the sugar and secure with an elastic band. This handy little duster can be tapped on the surface for a very light dusting of sugar when making decorations and modelling.

Storecupboard ingredients

When you need a cake quickly, you want to be able to open the cupboard and have everything you need instantly to hand. The following ingredients are easy to source and should be kept in stock in your cupboards year-round!

Butter

It makes very little difference to the end result whether you use salted or unsalted (sweet) butter. I tend to use salted, as it is usually the cheaper of the two. Allow the butter to come to room temperature for a couple of hours before baking. If you've forgotten to do this or just haven't had time, dice the butter into small pieces and place in the microwave on a low power for 30 seconds.

Caster (superfine) sugar

Try not to use granulated (table) sugar for baking, as the crystals do not dissolve as readily and you can end up with a grainy texture to your cakes and cookies. If you have no caster (superfine) sugar, place your granulated (table) sugar in a food processor and blitz lightly to reduce the size of the grains before using.

Flours

My recipes require both plain (all-purpose) and self-raising (self-rising) flours. If you only have plain (all-purpose) flour, you can add a teaspoon or two of baking powder, but the results may be a bit hit-and-miss. As long as your flour is good quality and fresh it shouldn't need sifting (good news for busy girls!).

Eggs

My recipes always use large (US extra large) free-range eggs, which are my preferred choice for baking. Always break eggs cleanly into a separate bowl to ensure that no shell gets into the mixture.

Bicarbonate of soda (baking soda)

This is not only a raising (leavening) agent, but also reacts with the natural acidity in a recipe and intensifies the flavour and darkness of the cocoa.

Cocoa powder (unsweetened cocoa)

Try out different types of cocoa until you find a brand you are happy with. Ideally it needs to be a good dark colour and flavoursome, otherwise chocolate cakes are too pale and poor in taste. It doesn't need to be expensive to be of good quality.

Milk

Semi-skimmed (-skim) and whole milk is preferable for baking giving a much richer consistency than skimmed (skim) milk.

Malt vinegar (alegar)

This is used in combination with milk to replace buttermilk, which can be difficult to source.

Dried fruit

Try soaking your fruit in a little alcohol or hot water overnight to plump it up and improve its tenderness before you bake with it. If you have forgotten to do this, or if time is short, add the fruit to a pan with a little hot water and heat gently for ten minutes until the fruit is plump and the water has been absorbed.

Ground mixed spice (apple pie spice)

This gives fruit cakes a warm, spicy flavour and a truly scrumptious scent.

Icing (confectioners' or powdered) sugar

You will need this to make buttercream and royal icing, and for dusting the work surface to make it non-stick. Sift to remove any lumps before use.

Sugarpaste (rolled fondant) icing

This is the basis for all the cake and cookie designs in this book. It is possible to make your own but it is a complicated process and far too time-consuming for us busy girls! Visit the baking aisle of your local supermarket to pick up ready-made sugarpaste. White is the only colour you'll need, as this can be coloured to any shade you want at home (see Colouring).

Get Baking

Cake and icing recipes to make
your mouth water…

Preparing tins

When baking a large cake to decorate, it is important to prepare your tins (pans). Lining the sides and base of tins prevents the cake from sticking, and good, complete edges are required for the best decorated cake. It also helps the cake to retain moisture.

How to line a tin (pan)

1 Draw around the base of your tin onto greaseproof (wax) paper.
2 Cut out the circle, just inside the line so that it will sit neatly in the base of the tin.

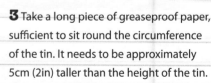

3 Take a long piece of greaseproof paper, sufficient to sit round the circumference of the tin. It needs to be approximately 5cm (2in) taller than the height of the tin.
4 Fold up 2.5cm (1in) from the base along the length of the paper and unfold.
5 Snip into the marked strip at 2cm (¾in) intervals all the way along.
6 Grease the cake tin lightly with a little butter or oil.
7 Fit the long length of lining into the tin around the outside edge. The snipped section should sit flush on the base of the tin.
8 Add the circular piece of greaseproof paper to the base of the tin and fill with the cake mixture.

TIP

When filling tins (pans), try not to get the mixture up the sides. This will quickly burn in the oven during baking and the smell will trick you into thinking your cake is burning!

Recipes

Before we can decorate we need to bake something delicious! You can use your own recipe or use one of these to get started.

Madeira cake

The quantities given in the chart opposite will create a cake approximately 4cm (1½in) in height once levelled. For a deeper cake than this, bake two (one at a time), level and stack together when filling (see Levelling and filling a sponge cake). Baking the cakes separately means that the baking time doesn't turn into hours on end and the crust stays nice and pale. Trust me, piling double mixture into one tin (pan) won't save you time!

TIP
Madeira cake can be kept in an airtight container, ideally in the fridge, for up to two weeks. To freeze, wrap well in cling film (plastic wrap) and store in the freezer for up to three months.

Madeira cake quantities

ROUND	15cm (6in)	18cm (7in)	20cm (8in)	23cm (9in)	25cm (10in)	28cm (11in)	30.5cm (12in)
SQUARE	13cm (5in)	15cm (6in)	18cm (7in)	20cm (8in)	23cm (9in)	25cm (10in)	28cm (11in)
Butter, softened	130g (4½oz)	200g (7oz)	250g (8¾oz)	300g (10½oz)	400g (14oz)	600g (1lb 5oz)	700g (1½lb)
Caster (superfine) sugar	130g (4½oz)	200g (7oz)	250g (8¾oz)	300g (10½oz)	400g (14oz)	600g (1lb 5oz)	700g (1½lb)
Eggs	2	4	5	6	8	9	10
Plain (all-purpose) flour	110g (3¾oz)	150g (5¼oz)	180g (6½oz)	220g (7¾oz)	300g (10½oz)	450g (1lb)	530g (1lb 2¾oz)
Self-raising (-rising) flour	30g (1oz)	50g (1¾oz)	60g (2oz)	75g (2¾oz)	95g (3½oz)	150g (5¼oz)	175g (6oz)
Milk	30ml (2 tbsp)	37.5ml (2½ tbsp)	45ml (3 tbsp)	52.5ml (3½ tbsp)	60ml (4 tbsp)	90ml (6 tbsp)	105ml (7 tbsp)
Baking time	1hr	1hr 15min	1hr 25min	1hr 35min	1hr 40min	1hr 55min	2hr 10min
Serves (cut into 5 x 2.5cm / 2 x 1in slices)	12	17	23	29	35	42	50

Method

1 Preheat the oven to 140ºC (fan)/160ºC/325ºF/Gas 3 and line the base and sides of the tin (pan) (see Preparing tins).

2 Cream together the softened butter and sugar until light and fluffy.

3 Beat in the eggs one by one until fully incorporated. Add a spoonful of flour at any sign of the mixture curdling, then fold in the remainder of the flours. Add the milk and stir through.

4 Pour the mixture into the lined tin (pan) and smooth the surface then bake in the oven for the time indicated in the chart above.

5 Cool in the tin (pan) for five minutes before removing and allowing to cool completely on a wire rack.

"Fold in the flour carefully until just incorporated and the batter is smooth. Don't beat the life out of it otherwise it will create large air bubbles in your cake!"

Chocolate cake

This chocolate cake recipe is brilliantly moist and lovely! The milk and vinegar combination replicates buttermilk, which can be hard to find (life's too short to hunt for buttermilk!). This recipe makes a fairly deep cake so you should only need one for the complete cake. Chocolate cake will keep well wrapped in an airtight container, ideally in the fridge, for up to one week. It can be kept frozen for three months.

TIP
The base of your baked cake will become the top when decorating it. To avoid the cooling rack indenting marks as it cools, flip the cake upside down to cool.

Chocolate cake quantities

ROUND	15cm (6in)	18cm (7in)	20cm (8in)	23cm (9in)	25cm (10in)	28cm (11in)	30.5cm (12in)	
SQUARE	13cm (5in)	15cm (6in)	18cm (7in)	20cm (8in)	23cm (9in)	25cm (10in)	28cm (11in)	30.5cm (12in)
Butter, softened	90g (3oz)	140g (5oz)	165g (5¾oz)	185g (6½oz)	225g (8oz)	325g (11½oz)	465g (1lb ½oz)	560g (1lb 3¾oz)
Caster (super-fine) sugar	165g (5¾oz)	250g (8¾oz)	300g (10½oz)	330g (11½oz)	410g (14½oz)	570g (1¼lb)	660g (1lb 7¼oz)	825g (1lb 13oz)
Eggs	2	2	3	3	4	5	6	7
Self-raising (-rising) flour	40g (1½oz)	50g (1¾oz)	60g (2oz)	70g (2½oz)	90g (3oz)	125g (4½oz)	150g (5¼oz)	190g (6¾oz)
Plain (all-purpose) flour	120g (4¼oz)	170g (6oz)	200g (7oz)	230g (8oz)	280g (9¾oz)	350g (12¼oz)	450g (1lb)	560g (1lb 3¾oz)
Bicarbonate of soda (baking soda)	2.5ml (½ tsp)	3.75ml (¾ tsp)	5ml (1 tsp)	6.25ml (1¼ tsp)	7.5ml (1½ tsp)	11.25ml (2¼ tsp)	12.5ml (2½ tsp)	13.75ml (2¾ tsp)
Cocoa powder (unsweetened cocoa)	40g (1½oz)	60g (2oz)	70g (2½oz)	80g (2¾oz)	90g (3oz)	110g (3¾oz)	120g (4¼oz)	160g (5½oz)
Milk	120ml (4fl oz)	200ml (7fl oz)	220ml (7½fl oz)	250ml (8½fl oz)	300ml (10fl oz)	440ml (15fl oz)	490ml (16½fl oz)	610ml (21fl oz)
Malt vinegar (alegar)	15ml (1 tbsp)	15ml (1 tbsp)	30ml (2 tbsp)	30ml (2 tbsp)	45ml (3 tbsp)	60ml (4 tbsp)	75ml (5 tbsp)	90ml (6 tbsp)
Baking time	50min	1hr	1hr 10min	1hr 15min	1hr 20min	1hr 30min	1hr 40min	1hr 50min
Serves (cut into 5 x 2.5cm / 2 x 1in slices)	12	17	23	29	35	42	50	60

Method

1 Preheat the oven to 160ºC (fan)/180ºC/350ºF/Gas 4 and line the base and sides of the tin (pan) (see Preparing tins).

2 Combine the vinegar and milk in a jug and set to one side.

3 Cream together the softened butter and sugar until light and fluffy.

4 Beat in the eggs one by one until fully incorporated. Add a spoonful of flour at any sign of the mixture curdling.

5 Add the remaining ingredients – flour, cocoa, soda and the milk/vinegar mixture – and beat well until smooth.

6 Pour the mixture into the lined tin (pan) and smooth the surface then bake in the oven for the time indicated in the chart above.

7 Cool in the tin (pan) for five minutes before removing and allowing to cool completely on a wire rack.

Fruit cake

A delicious fruit cake makes a firm stable base for decorating. It can be made (and decorated) well in advance, as it keeps very well. Fruit cake can be stored well wrapped in a cool dry place for six months or frozen for three years.

> ## TIP
> Very few ovens operate true to temperature. To reduce the risk of large cakes burning, or taking twice the stated baking time, a removable oven thermometer is a really useful piece of kit.

Method

1 Mix together the dried fruit and brandy. Cover and allow to soak for a couple of hours or overnight. When time is short, warm the brandy gently first in a small pan. This encourages the dried fruit to absorb the liquid much more quickly.

2 Preheat the oven to 130ºC (fan)/140ºC/ 275ºF/Gas 1 and line the base and sides of the tin (pan) (see Preparing tins).

3 Beat together the butter and sugar, add the eggs one by one adding a little flour at any sign of curdling. Then add the remaining flour and spices and mix well.

4 In a large bowl, combine the soaked fruit and the cake mixture. Ensure the fruit is evenly distributed before placing into your lined tin (pan). Give the filled tin (pan) a couple of sharp taps on your work surface to knock out any air bubbles, which will leave holes in your cake.

5 Bake in the oven for the time indicated in the chart opposite.

6 Remove from the oven and allow to cool in the tin (pan). Once completely cooled, remove from the tin (pan) and wrap tightly in cling film (plastic wrap) until required.

Fruit cake quantities

ROUND	15cm (6in)	18cm (7in)	20cm (8in)	23cm (9in)	25cm (10in)	28cm (11in)	30.5cm (12in)	
SQUARE	13cm (5in)	15cm (6in)	18cm (7in)	20cm (8in)	23cm (9in)	25cm (10in)	28cm (11in)	30.5cm (12in)
Sultanas (golden raisins)	325g (11½oz)	445g (15¾oz)	615g (1lb 5¾oz)	780g (1lb 11½oz)	1.1kg (2lb 6¾oz)	1.3kg (2lb 13¾oz)	1.6kg (3½lb)	1.85kg (4lb 1¼oz)
Raisins	120g (4¼oz)	170g (6oz)	250g (8¾oz)	300g (10½oz)	410g (14½oz)	500g (1lb 1½oz)	610g (1lb 5½oz)	725g (1lb 9½oz)
Currants (small raisins)	40g (1½oz)	70g (2½oz)	100g (3½oz)	120g (4¼oz)	165g (5¾oz)	200g (7oz)	245g (8¾oz)	290g (10¼oz)
Brandy	40ml (2½ tbsp)	40ml (2½ tbsp)	40ml (2½ tbsp)	60ml (4 tbsp)	60ml (4 tbsp)	80ml (5½ tbsp)	120ml (8 tbsp)	160ml (10½ tbsp)
Butter	100g (3½oz)	150g (5¼oz)	200g (7oz)	275g (9¾oz)	410g (14½oz)	475g (1lb ¾oz)	560g (1lb 3¾oz)	700g (1½lb)
Soft (light) brown sugar	100g (3½oz)	150g (5¼oz)	200g (7oz)	275g (9¾oz)	410g (14½oz)	475g (1lb ¾oz)	560g (1lb 3¾oz)	700g (1½lb)
Eggs	2	3	3	4	6	8	8	10
Plain (all-purpose) flour	125g (4½oz)	185g (6½oz)	250g (8¾oz)	375g (13¼oz)	500g (1lb 1½oz)	625g (1lb 6oz)	750g (1lb 10½oz)	875g (1lb 14¾oz)
Mixed spice (apple pie spice)	2.5ml (½ tsp)	5ml (1 tsp)	7.5ml (1½ tsp)	10ml (2 tsp)	15ml (3 tsp)	20ml (4 tsp)	20ml (4 tsp)	25ml (5 tsp)
Baking time	2hr	2hr 30min	3hr	3hr 30min	4hr	4hr 30min	5hr	5hr 30min
Serves (cut into 5 x 2.5cm / 2 x 1in slices)	24	34	46	58	70	85	100	120

Vanilla cupcakes

These cupcakes are quick to whip up and are extremely versatile for decorating.

Ingredients (for 12 cupcakes):

- 200g (7oz) butter, softened
- 200g (7oz) caster (superfine) sugar
- 5ml (1 tsp) vanilla extract
- 4 large (US extra large) eggs
- 200g (7oz) self-raising (-rising) flour
- 15ml (1 tbsp) milk

Method

1 Preheat the oven to 160ºC (fan)/180ºC/ 350ºF/Gas 4 and line a cupcake tray with cupcake cases.

2 Cream together the softened butter and sugar until light and fluffy.

3 Add the vanilla extract then beat in the eggs one by one until fully incorporated. Add a spoonful of flour at any sign of the mixture curdling, then fold in the remainder of the flours. Finally stir the milk through the mixture.

4 Fill the cupcake cases two-thirds full.

5 Bake in the oven for 18–20 minutes until they are lightly golden and springy to the touch.

6 Cool the cupcakes in the tray for five minutes before removing and allowing to cool completely on a wire rack.

TIP

A spring-loaded ice-cream/ cookie scoop makes filling cupcake cases wonderfully easy. It measures the perfectly even amount of mixture into every case and makes for super-speedy case filling!

Chocolate cupcakes

When you need a chocolate fix only a chocolate cupcake will do! Lovely moist chocolate sponge makes the ideal base for your decorating project.

Ingredients (for 12 cupcakes):

- 70g (2½oz) butter, softened
- 125g (4½oz) caster (superfine) sugar
- 1 large (US extra large) egg
- 25g (¾oz) self-raising (-rising) flour
- 85g (3oz) plain (all-purpose) flour
- 2.5ml (½ tsp) bicarbonate of soda (baking soda)
- 40g (1½oz) cocoa powder (unsweetened cocoa)
- 80ml (5½ tbsp) milk
- 7.5ml (1½ tsp) malt vinegar (alegar)

Method

1 Preheat the oven to 160ºC (fan)/180ºC/350ºF/ Gas 4 and line a cupcake tray with cupcake cases.

2 Combine the vinegar and milk in a jug and set to one side.

3 Cream together the softened butter and sugar until light and fluffy.

4 Beat in the eggs one by one until fully incorporated. Add a spoonful of flour at any sign of the mixture curdling

5 Add the remainder of the flours, cocoa, soda and the milk/vinegar mixture and beat well.

6 Fill the cupcake cases two-thirds full.

7 Bake in the oven for 18–20 minutes until they are springy to the touch.

8 Cool the cupcakes in the tray for five minutes before removing and allowing to cool completely on a wire rack.

Lemon cupcakes

Zingy lemon cupcakes are my favourite. Why not try a batch? I'm sure they'll be a favourite with you too!

Ingredients (for 12 cupcakes):

- 200g (7oz) butter, softened
- 200g (7oz) caster (superfine) sugar
- 4 large (US extra large) eggs
- 175g (6oz) self-raising (-rising) flour
- 5ml (1 tsp) baking powder
- Zest and juice of 1 lemon

Method

1 Preheat the oven to 160ºC (fan)/180ºC/350ºF/Gas 4 and line a cupcake tray with cupcake cases.

2 Cream together the softened butter and sugar until light and fluffy. Add the lemon zest and beat well.

3 Beat in the eggs one by one until fully incorporated. Add a spoonful of flour at any sign of the mixture curdling, then fold in the remaining flour and the baking powder.

4 Stir in the lemon juice and mix well.

5 Fill the cupcake cases two-thirds full.

6 Bake in the oven for 18–20 minutes until they are lightly golden and springy to the touch.

7 Cool the cupcakes in the tray for five minutes before removing and allowing to cool completely on a wire rack.

Blackberry cupcakes

Fruity cupcakes are always moist and delicious – any seasonal fruit can be substituted for the blackberries if you prefer. These are best eaten within two days of baking.

Ingredients (for 12 cupcakes):

- 150g (5¼oz) butter, softened
- 150g (5¼oz) caster (superfine) sugar
- 3 large (US extra large) eggs
- 150g (5¼oz) self-raising (-rising) flour
- 100g (3½oz) blackberries

Method

1 Preheat the oven to 160ºC (fan)/180ºC/350ºF/Gas 4 and line a cupcake tray with cupcake cases.

2 Cream together the softened butter and sugar until light and fluffy.

3 Beat in the eggs one by one until fully incorporated. Add a spoonful of flour at any sign of the mixture curdling, then fold in the remaining flour.

4 Gently stir through the blackberries trying not to smash them into little bits!

5 Fill the cupcake cases two-thirds full.

6 Bake in the oven for 18–20 minutes until they are lightly golden and springy to the touch.

7 Cool the cupcakes in the tray for five minutes before removing and allowing to cool completely on a wire rack.

TIP

Cakes made with fresh fruit will not last as long as those without due to the extra moisture the fruit provides.

Vanilla sugar cookies

These cookies are the perfect base for decorating – they keep their shape well and have a beautifully smooth texture.

Ingredients (for 24 cookies, approx 5cm/2½in)

- 225g (8oz) butter, softened
- 225g (8oz) caster (superfine) sugar
- 1 large (US extra large) egg
- 5ml (1 tsp) vanilla bean paste (or the seeds of 1 vanilla pod, or 5ml/1 tsp vanilla extract)
- 375g (13¼oz) plain (all-purpose) flour

Method

1 Preheat the oven to 160ºC (fan)/180ºC/350ºF/Gas 4. Grease or line a baking tray.

2 Cream together the butter and sugar until light and fluffy.

3 Add the egg and vanilla and mix well. Add the flour and thoroughly mix to form a dough.

4 Split the dough in half. Roll out each half between two sheets of greaseproof (wax) paper to approx 4mm (⅛in) thick and place in the fridge to chill for 30 minutes or until firm.

5 Cut out the cookies using your chosen cutter. Place on the greased or lined baking tray, chill again for a further 15 minutes or until they are completely hard again. The chilling stops the cookies from spreading and will help them keep their shape while baking.

6 Keep re-rolling the scraps, cutting and chilling again between two sheets of greaseproof (wax) paper until you have used up all the dough.

7 Bake in the oven for approximately 10 minutes until the cookies are golden brown on the edges.

8 Remove from the oven and allow to cool on the tray. If the cookies have spread out of shape, re-cut them with your cutter or a knife while still warm.

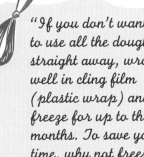

"If you don't want to use all the dough straight away, wrap well in cling film (plastic wrap) and freeze for up to three months. To save you time, why not freeze it ready rolled out between two sheets of greaseproof (wax) paper?"

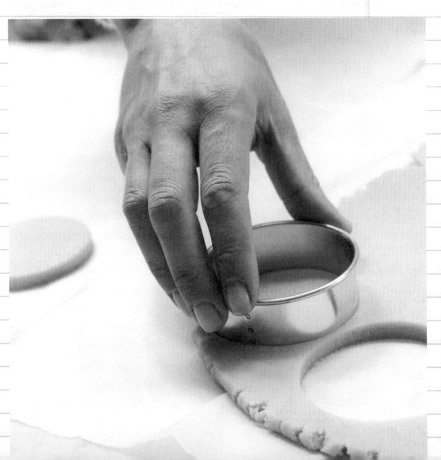

Buttercream

This is a cake decorator's staple. Sweet and creamy, it can be used in all sorts of ways – to fill and even out a cake, piped or spread onto cupcakes – and helps to keep cakes moist and delicious.

Ingredients (for enough to pipe swirls on 12 cupcakes or 24 if coating with a palette knife, or to fill a 20cm/8in cake)

- 250g (8¾oz) butter, softened
- 500g (1lb 1½oz) icing (confectioners') sugar, sifted
- 15–30ml (1–2 tbsp) milk to reach a smooth soft buttercream (the consistency should be firm enough to still hold its shape but soft enough to spread or pipe easily)

"Buttercream is so quick and easy, you can even make it in a mixer or food processor – just make sure your butter is nice and soft and start mixing very slowly, otherwise you'll cover the kitchen (and yourself) in a cloud of sugar!"

Method

1 Beat together the softened butter and icing (confectioners') sugar.
2 Add the milk until the buttercream reaches the desired consistency.
3 For flavoured buttercream, add essences such as coffee, lemon or orange in place of the milk.

TIP

Buttercream can be kept frozen for three months if you're not using it right away. Allow to defrost in the fridge the day before needed and beat well just prior to using.

Chocolate frosting

This is a rich and decadent frosting, which is ideal for a luxurious cake.

Ingredients (for enough to pipe swirls on 12 cupcakes or 24 if coating with a palette knife, or to fill a 20cm/8in cake)

- 200ml (7fl oz) double (heavy) cream
- 200g (7oz) dark (semisweet) chocolate
- 250g (8¾oz) icing (confectioners') sugar, sifted

Method

1 Chop the chocolate roughly.

2 Heat the cream in a pan until just below boiling. Remove from the heat.

3 Add the chocolate and allow to stand for two minutes.

4 Stir to a smooth glossy ganache.

5 Allow to cool fully to room temperature. The ganache needs to be fully set before adding the sugar.

6 Beat in the sifted icing (confectioners') sugar until smooth.

TIP

Chocolate with a high percentage cocoa solids content gives the best flavour, but make sure it's a cook's chocolate otherwise the ganache may split.

"If you're in a hurry why not use shop-bought frosting? There are lots of variations available and then you're ready to go without the fuss."

Royal icing

Royal icing is glossy, shiny and sets hard, so that your piped dots and lines stay exactly as they should. Consistency is the key to working with royal icing. You can make it firmer by adding more icing (confectioners') sugar and looser by adding a little extra water, a tiny drop at a time. The desired consistency should be that when you apply pressure to the piping (pastry) bag the icing will flow gently from the nozzle (tip). You shouldn't struggle to squeeze the bag – if you are, the icing is too firm. Always sift the icing (confectioners') sugar to remove any lumps.

Ingredients

- 500g (1lb 1½oz) icing (confectioners') sugar, sifted
- 15ml (1 tbsp) powdered egg white (such as Meri-White)
- 60–80ml (4–5½ tbsp) water
- Edible gel paste colour

"Royal icing box mixes are also a good cupboard staple, allowing you to mix up as much or as little as you need."

Method

1 Mix together all the ingredients to the desired consistency, adding more water if needed.

2 Beat a little gel paste colour into the white royal icing. Allow to stand for a couple of minutes to allow the colour to develop then beat again before using.

3 Once you have made it, stop the royal icing from drying out by placing a clean, damp tea towel over the bowl.

TIP

Using freshly made royal icing is preferable, but it will keep in an airtight container at room temperature for a couple of days. Make sure you beat it well before use.

Get Decorating

Techniques and know-how
to build your confidence...

Techniques

Once you have mastered the basic techniques you'll be all set to go – practice makes perfect so do keep trying if you find something difficult at first.

Piping

Different types of work with royal icing require slightly different consistencies. For piping lines, royal icing should be on the stiffer side, but not so stiff that it hurts your hand when squeezing the bag. For dots and snail trails you will need a slightly wetter consistency but it should still hold its shape when piped.

Adjust the consistency by adding more water or icing (confectioners') sugar. It is worth spending the time getting the right consistency, as it will make your work much easier. Time spent now equals time saved later!

Preparing and filling a piping (pastry) bag

1 Snip 1.5cm (½in) from the end of a piping (pastry) bag and drop in the piping nozzle (tip) you are using. Pull the nozzle (tip) down into the end of the bag so that it sits tightly.

2 To fill, insert the end of the bag into a glass or a jug and fold the end of the bag over the outside. It's now super easy to fill with royal icing.

3 Once filled, remove from the glass or jug. Squeeze the icing down towards the nozzle (tip) and twist the bag behind it to stop it from leaking out. Take care not to overfill the bag otherwise you'll end up in a sticky mess!

4 Hold the bag in your dominant hand, laying it across your palm between your thumb and forefinger. Grip the bag with your hand and apply pressure from the top down towards the nozzle (tip). Support the tip of the bag lightly with the forefinger of your opposite hand. You are now ready to pipe!

Piping lines

1 To pipe a line of royal icing, first make sure there are no air bubbles in your piping (pastry) bag – by squeezing the icing downwards in the bag towards the nozzle (tip) – as these will break the line and ruin your hard work.

2 Position your nozzle (tip) just above your piping starting point. Apply an even pressure to the bag. As the icing starts to flow, allow it to 'attach' to the starting point on your cake. Continually applying pressure, lift the bag up vertically away from the cake so that you are holding a line of icing 2–3cm (¾–1¼in) long.

3 Keeping the pressure applied, move horizontally in the direction of the line, maintain the vertical position and 'lay' down the icing exactly where you wish it to go. Naturally you will want to keep the line down close to the cake but the higher position gives you control of the piping and not the other way round! To finish, drop the line back down to the cake gently touching the nozzle (tip) down to secure the end of the line to the cake.

Piping a snail trail

1 To pipe a snail trail, fit the piping (pastry) bag with your required nozzle (tip) and fill the bag as described on the previous page.

2 Hold the nozzle (tip) at a 45-degree angle to the cake in your starting position. Keeping the position still, squeeze the bag until the royal icing forms the size of bulb you are looking for. Release the pressure, stopping the squeeze and then pull the bag away in the direction of the snail trail. This will form the tail of the bulb.

3 Position the nozzle (tip) 5mm (³⁄₁₆in) from the first tailed bulb and repeat the process. Squeeze the bag until the bulb joins the previous tail, release the pressure to stop piping and pull the piping bag away to create the next tail. Repeat all the way around the cake.

TIP
If making a snail trail around the base of a cake, always start at the back.

Piping a shell border

1 To pipe a shell border, fit the piping (pastry) bag with a no. 8 or no. 43 star nozzle (tip) and fill the bag as described on the previous page.

2 Hold the tip of the bag at a 45-degree angle to the cake in your starting position. Keeping the position still, squeeze the bag until the royal icing forms the size of shell you are looking for. Release the pressure, stopping the squeeze and then pull the bag away in the direction of the border.

3 Position the nozzle (tip) 5mm (³⁄₁₆in) from the first shell shape and repeat the process. Squeeze the bag until the shell joins the previous one and then pull away in the direction you are moving. Repeat all the way around the cake.

Piping swirls

1 To pipe buttercream swirls onto the tops of cupcakes, first prepare a batch of buttercream (see Buttercream).

2 Fit a large piping (pastry) bag with a large open star nozzle (tip) (Wilton 1M) and fill the bag as described on the previous page. Squeeze the buttercream down the bag towards the nozzle (tip).

3 Hold the bag as you would a smaller royal icing piping (pastry) bag in your leading hand. Position the tip hovering just above the cupcake at the outside edge of the cake.

4 Apply an even pressure to the bag and start to pipe the buttercream, moving in a circular motion around the outside edge of the cupcake as the buttercream flows. Move around the cupcake in one continuous motion in decreasing circles until you reach the centre.

5 Keeping the nozzle (tip) in the centre, release the pressure to stop the buttercream flow and the lift the bag upwards and away.

Making a mini-cake

Miniature tins (pans) can be bought to bake evenly sized mini-cakes, however they are expensive. A much easier way of creating mini-cakes is to bake a sheet cake and cut and stack smaller circles.

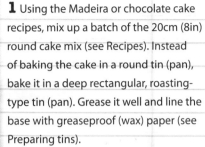

1 Using the Madeira or chocolate cake recipes, mix up a batch of the 20cm (8in) round cake mix (see Recipes). Instead of baking the cake in a round tin (pan), bake it in a deep rectangular, roasting-type tin (pan). Grease it well and line the base with greaseproof (wax) paper (see Preparing tins).

2 Bake in a preheated oven at 160ºC (fan)/180ºC/350ºF/Gas 4 for approximately 35 minutes until cooked and slightly springy to the touch.

3 Allow to cool slightly in the tin (pan) before inverting the cake onto a wire rack to cool completely.

4 Once cooled, chill the cake in the fridge and then cut out 6cm (2.5in) circles using a straight-edged round cutter. Use two or three cut outs to create each cake, levelling and filling as you would a large cake (see opposite).

"Chilling the cake before cutting it means that you will get a good straight cut for the edges of the mini-cake. The cake won't crumble like it does when it is at room temperature."

Levelling and filling a sponge cake

Madeira and chocolate cakes need to be fully cooled before attempting to split them, otherwise you will end up with a pile of crumbs! In fact, chilling your cake will help when levelling it and cutting it into layers.

1 Take the tin (pan) used to bake the cake in and drop in a stack of small cake boards or a small bowl to lift the cake to the correct height. Carefully drop the cake back in. Adjust the height the cake sits at up or down as necessary. Keeping the blade of a serrated knife level with the top edge of the tin (pan), slice off the top of the cake so that it is perfectly level.

2 Remove the cake from the tin (pan) and adjust the height of the boards inside so that the cake can be split in the middle. Place the cake back in the tin (pan) and split through the middle. Scoring around the edge of the cake will help give you an even cut.

3 Flip the cake out of the tin taking care to keep it in one piece. The bottom should now be on the top. Insert two cocktail sticks (toothpicks) aligned vertically, one in each cake layer.

4 Place the cake onto a plate or board. Remove the top layer and fill with buttercream (see Buttercream) and jam as desired. Replace the top layer using the cocktail stick (toothpick) markers to align.

5 Using a palette knife, coat the top of the cake with buttercream. Then coat around the edge of the cake, working the buttercream around the sides from the top down to the base. Using the blade of the palette knife, scrape the excess buttercream from the cake to give a smooth finish.

6 Remove the cocktail sticks (toothpicks) and finally finish this area. Smooth the buttercream join at the top edge. Check with your eye that the cake is level. Chill hard in the fridge before covering with sugarpaste (rolled fondant) (see Covering a cake with sugarpaste).

Covering a fruit cake with marzipan

Fruit cakes benefit from a layer of marzipan to help seal in their moistness and flavour and to act as a barrier to stop the fruit staining the sugarpaste (rolled fondant). It also provides a level surface for the sugarpaste.

1 Cover the cake in a thin layer of apricot jam or marmalade using a pastry brush. Zap it in the microwave for 30 seconds to soften if it needs it. This will be the 'glue' to hold on the marzipan layer.

2 To cover a 20cm (8in) cake, 500g (1lb 1½oz) of marzipan is enough. If you love the taste of marzipan you can make this layer thicker but you will need more to do so. Lightly dust your work surface with a little icing (confectioners') sugar. Knead the marzipan gently to warm and soften it, making it easier to work with.

3 Take half of the marzipan and shape into a rough sausage shape. Keeping your surface lightly dusted with icing (confectioners') sugar roll out the sausage into a long strip, 4mm (⅛in) thick, to reach around the circumference of the cake. Measure the cake with string to help determine the length and width it needs to be.

4 Position the collar around the outside of the cake, ensuring that the marzipan sits neatly at the base. Trim neatly where the two edges meet using a sharp knife. If the collar protrudes above the cake, trim it level with a pair of scissors.

5 Gather together the trimmings and the remaining half of marzipan and roll out to 4mm (⅛in) thick on your work surface. Using the tin (pan) you baked the cake in as a template, cut out a circle for the top of the cake.

6 Place the circle on the top of the cake, gently sealing together the edges where it meets the marzipan collar. Use your hands to smooth the seams of the marzipan. Smooth the top and the sides, working out any major lumps and bumps. Repeat with an icing smoother.

TIP
Marzipan layers appreciate 24–48 hours to dry out slightly, which will provide a firmer surface to support the sugarpaste layer.

"It's frustrating to find your marzipan or sugarpaste has stuck to your work surface. Check it frequently and dust with a little more icing (confectioners') sugar if necessary."

Covering a cake with sugarpaste

Sugarpaste (rolled fondant) finishes a cake with a smooth polished surface and provides the very best canvas to work on when creating beautiful cake designs.

1 If covering a sponge cake, the cake needs to be chilled hard to set the buttercream. On removing from the fridge, shave off any lumps and bumps using a sharp knife. Set the cake on a plate or spare cake board. If covering a fruit cake, lightly spray the marzipan covering with a mist of water if the cake is to be served right away. If the cake is to be kept for any length of time it is best to use a clear alcohol such as vodka.

2 Roll out the sugarpaste on your work surface lightly dusted with icing (confectioners') sugar, trying to keep it in a circular shape and at an even thickness of 5mm (³⁄₁₆in). Measure the size of your cake with a piece of string and use to compare to your sugarpaste. Trim off any excess – if one side is far too long the weight of the overhang will pull and crack as it is laid onto the cake.

3 Once the sugarpaste is rolled out to the correct size, use an icing smoother to polish it on the work surface. Then lift the sugarpaste using your rolling pin and lay it centrally onto the cake.

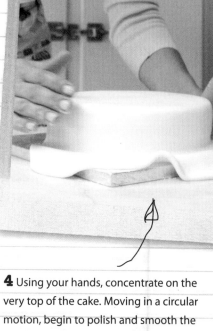

4 Using your hands, concentrate on the very top of the cake. Moving in a circular motion, begin to polish and smooth the sugarpaste. Cup your hands and polish again around the very top edge. Now turn your attention to the sides, gently working your way down the cake towards the base. Lift the sugarpaste out from the bottom, as if smoothing out a skirt, to encourage the sugarpaste to the cover the cake flat, lifting out any creases.

5 Once the sugarpaste is smoothed all the way down the sides, use an icing smoother to polish the surface. At the base of the cake, press down the smoother to start to form a mark where the sugarpaste can be trimmed.

TIP

Before starting, remove all rings, bracelets and watches – they will mark the sugarpaste and ruin your cake from the outset!

6 Using a sharp knife, cut cleanly around the base of the cake to cut away the excess sugarpaste and remove.

7 Use your hands and the smoother to finish off the cut edge. Set to one side and allow to dry before decorating.

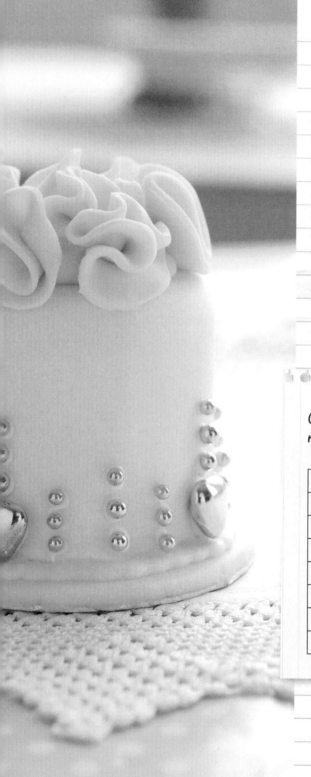

Covering a mini-cake

1 To cover a mini-cake, roll out a square of sugarpaste (rolled fondant) as you would for a larger cake, however it will only need to be approximately 16cm (6¼in) round. Use to cover the mini-cake as described for a larger cake (see Covering a cake with sugarpaste).
2 Because of their size it is often easier to polish the icing using two smoothers, one in each hand on either side of the mini-cake.

Quantities of sugarpaste (rolled fondant) needed to cover a cake

SIZE	ROUND	SQUARE
15cm (6in)	600g (1lb 5oz)	650g (1½lb)
18cm (7in)	800g (1¾lb)	900g (2lb)
20cm (8in)	1kg (2¼lb)	1.2kg (2½lb)
23cm (9in)	1.2kg (2½lb)	1.4kg (3lb)
25cm (10in)	1.4kg (3lb)	1.75kg (3¾lb)
28cm (11in)	1.75kg (3¾lb)	1.9kg (4lb 3oz)
30.5cm (12in)	2.2kg (4¾lb)	2.25kg (5lb)

Covering a board with sugarpaste

Covering a cake board in sugarpaste (rolled fondant) before mounting your cake makes the whole project look much more professional. Always cover boards if you have the time, they can be decorated to match your cake too!

1 Roll out the sugarpaste to a depth of 3mm (⅛in), measuring the size needed using string. While still flat on the work surface, polish using an icing smoother.
2 Lightly mist the cake board with a water spray.
3 Lift the sugarpaste using your rolling pin and lay down over the board. Polish again with the icing smoother.
4 Trim the excess sugarpaste from the board using a sharp knife in the same way you would trim excess pastry from a pie. Smooth the cut edge with the palm of your hand. Emboss if desired (see Embossing). Set to one side and allow to dry before decorating.

Trimming a board with ribbon

1 Run a length of double-sided tape around the edge of the board.
2 Fix the ribbon into place and secure at the back with a pearl-headed pin.

> **TIP**
> Water sprays are useful pieces of kit that can be picked up in little travel sets and are small and easy to store.

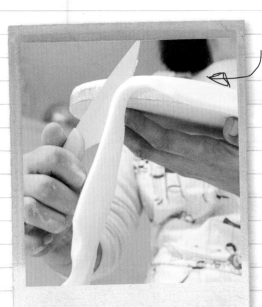

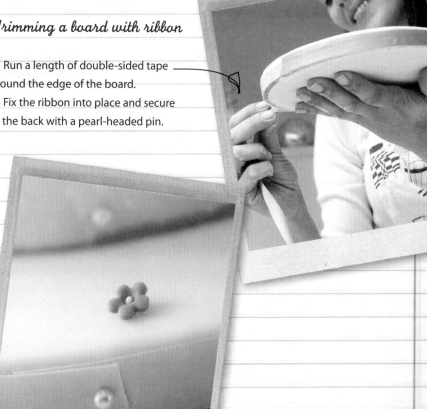

"To cover mini-cake boards, make life easier by matching the size of the cake card to that of a round cutter. Cut out the circle and adhere to the card – hey presto!"

Colouring

To colour sugarpaste (rolled fondant) and royal icing it is best to use edible gel paste colours. These colours are extremely concentrated. Recommended brands include Wilton, Sugarflair and Squires Kitchen (see Suppliers). Powder colours are used for dusting and can also be mixed with a little clear alcohol (vodka or gin) to form a paint, which can be applied with a brush. Liquid colours, available in supermarkets, are far less concentrated in colour and quickly change the consistency of sugarpaste or royal icing and so are best avoided.

Beware when needing strength in royal icing for line and lace work – gel paste colours contain glycerine, which can weaken the icing, so consider using a powder in this instance. A little gum tragacanth (often known as 'gum trag') can be beaten into royal icing to strengthen it. Use the chart, right, to mix specific colours.

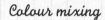

Colour mixing

Colour	Combination (in parts)
Red-orange	1 red + 3 orange
Baby pink	½ pink
Dusky pink	1 pink + ½ brown
Bright pink	3 pink
Pinky red	1 red + 1 pink
Fuchsia	1 purple + 2 pink
Soft yellow	1 yellow + ½ orange
Yellow orange	2 yellow + 2 orange
Flesh	½ pink + ½ yellow
Salmon	1 pink + 1 orange
Lime	2 green + 4 yellow
Sage	2 green + 1 brown
Leaf	4 green +1 brown + ½ blue
Teal	1 green + 1 blue
Baby blue	1 blue
Bright blue	3 blue
Dark blue	5 blue + 4 purple
Violet	1 blue + 1 purple
Mauve	½ purple + ½ pink
Lilac	1 purple
Deep purple	3 purple

The colour wheel

Many varied shades of sugarpaste can be achieved using just the three primary colours at the centre of the wheel, red, yellow and blue. Mixing equal amounts of each gel paste colour will create the colours within the middle ring. To create the shades in the outer ring, add an additional amount of one of the primary colours e.g. mixing a little blue with a lot of yellow will create a lime green colour.

How to colour sugarpaste (rolled fondant)

1 Knead white sugarpaste till soft and pliable on a work surface lightly dusted with icing (confectioners') sugar.

2 Form into a sausage shape and flatten. Using a cocktail stick (toothpick), add the gel paste colour to the centre of the flattened sugarpaste.

3 Pinch together the edges of the sugarpaste to seal the gel inside. Roll the sausage between your hands to begin to spread the gel from the middle out through the sausage. Keep folding the sausage to bury the colour into the middle again. Repeat until the colour is spread evenly through the sugarpaste.

4 Wrap in cling film (plastic wrap) and allow the colour to develop. Colour intensifies over a period of ten minutes or so. Unwrap and knead gently, checking that the colour is even. Your coloured sugarpaste is now ready to be used.

> **TIP**
> Alternatively you can wear latex gloves and knead the colour through the sugarpaste, but be careful not to stain your work surface.

Stacking a tiered cake

To support the top tier of a stacked cake and to stop it sinking into the lower layer and ruining all your decorating work, you will need to dowel the cake. To do this you will need four cake dowels. These come in a variety of forms but by far the best (and quickest) are plastic dowels.

"Remember to tell whoever the cake is for that the bottom tier contains plastic dowels so that they can be removed before serving!"

1 Take the bottom tier of your cake, ready covered and mounted on its board. Insert four dowels, equally spaced vertically down through the sugarpaste (rolled fondant) to the board. The position of the dowels needs to stay within the area of the smaller tier above so that they will not be seen.

2 Mark the dowels with a pen level with the surface of the sugarpaste.

3 Remove each dowel and lay side by side. With the ends of the dowels aligned, tape them together using a piece of masking tape. You will see that the marks are not all level, you need to work to the highest mark. This ensures that the tier will sit level and not wonky. Remark all the dowels to the same level.

4 Un-tape the dowels. Take a sharp knife and score on the marked position.

5 Holding each dowel in turn firmly between your two hands, 'snap' the dowels to the correct length. The snapping method is preferable to using a hacksaw or pair of snips as it creates a clean, level break in the dowel.

6 Re-insert each of the snapped dowels into the cake.

7 Spread a little royal icing or buttercream in the centre of the cake between the dowels.

8 The next tier must be mounted onto a cake card or board and be ready covered. Place the next tier on top of the first. You can repeat this method to create three, four or even five tiered cakes (though as we're busy girls, two tiers will suffice!).

1

2

3

4

TIP

If there is a slight gap
between the two tiers, this
can easily be covered by
clever positioning of a ribbon
or by adding decorations.

5

6

7

8

Making a wired cake topper

To create the wired fountains that adorn many beautiful cakes you will need a posy pick. These are pointed plastic holders that come in a variety of sizes and are safe to use with cakes. Never push wires directly into cake, as they will corrode and contaminate the cake.

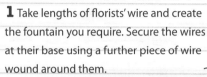

1 Take lengths of florists' wire and create the fountain you require. Secure the wires at their base using a further piece of wire wound around them.

2 Insert the wires into the posy pick. If they don't sit in there securely, take a small ball of sugarpaste (rolled fondant) and insert into the posy pick followed by the wires. This should hold it steady.

3 Constructing the fountain can be tricky – to hold it still, try inserting it into an apple or potato with the base cut level so that it sits steadily on your work surface.

4 When it's ready to be put into the cake, push the posy pick down vertically into the centre of your cake.

Embossing

Embossing sugarpaste (rolled fondant) involves pressing textured objects into the surface to leave an imprint. It is a simple yet effective way of texturing paste, creating intricate designs. The technique needs to be done on fresh sugarpaste, not dried.

1 Make sure your chosen object is either brand new or spotlessly clean and absolutely dry before use.

2 Lightly dust your chosen object with a little icing (confectioners') sugar – using a duster is ideal (see Equipment).

3 Press the object gently onto freshly rolled-out sugarpaste and then lift away. You should be left with a perfectly embossed design.

4 Dust the embossed pattern with edible lustre dust to highlight the design if desired.

> **TIP**
> Practise embossing on a piece of excess sugarpaste first to get a feel for the correct amount of pressure required.

Making a rolled rose

These simple and effective flowers are very quick and pretty for impromptu decorations.

1 Take a ball of sugarpaste (rolled fondant) approximately 7cm (2¾in) in diameter and shape by hand into a rough sausage shape.

2 Roll the shape out thinly on your work surface dusted lightly with icing (confectioners') sugar to stop it sticking. Once it is in a long rectangle, fold it in half widthways. Lightly press the two edges together leaving the top fold slightly puffy.

3 Still on the work surface, start to roll the flower up from one end. Once the roll is started, lift it up and hold it with your hands as you continue to roll up the flower.

4 Pinch off the excess sugarpaste from the base of the flower and set it aside.

Now Get Busy!

Twenty-five projects to motivate
and inspire you…

Evening Whip-Ups

Butterfly kisses

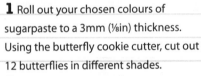

BUILDING A 3D DESIGN

These pastel butterfly cookies are stunning and easy to make too – why not whip up a batch for someone special?

Get it together...

- 12 butterfly cookies
- Sugarpaste: romantic colours of your choice e.g. peach, pale peach and pink
- Cutters: butterfly cookie and small butterfly
- Edible gold lustre dust
- Basic equipment (see Equipment)

1 Roll out your chosen colours of sugarpaste to a 3mm (⅛in) thickness. Using the butterfly cookie cutter, cut out 12 butterflies in different shades.

2 Brush the top of each cookie with a little water and attach the sugarpaste butterfly in place, pressing down lightly to secure.

3 Using the back of a knife, mark the veins on the butterfly's wings.

4 Roll out a complementary colour of sugarpaste to a 3mm (⅛in) thickness and cut out 12 smaller butterflies.

5 Mark the veins with the back of a knife and place on top of the larger butterfly, securing with a dab of water.

6 Roll out a small ball for the head and a tube for the body and position on top of each small butterfly.

7 Add a little sprinkle of gold lustre dust for an extra hint of sparkle.

"This project isn't as fiddly as it might sound – set up a production line doing each stage of the cookies in one go and you'll soon have a beautiful batch of Butterfly Kisses!"

Lavender lines

LAYERING CUT-OUT FLOWERS

Blossoms in subtly different shades create a stylish layered effect, which would work equally well on cupcakes as on cookies.

Get it together...

- 12 round cookies
- Sugarpaste: purple and white
- Cutters: round cookie, large and small blossoms
- Silver sugar dragees, medium and small
- Basic equipment (see Equipment)

TIP

Pick up the dragees using a dry paintbrush – the bristles will grab them, making it easy to lift them into place.

1 Take a ball of purple sugarpaste and knead into a ball of white sugarpaste the same size to create a pale purple colour.

2 Roll out the pale purple sugarpaste to a 3mm (⅛in) thickness. Using the round cookie cutter, cut out 12 circles.

3 Brush the top of each cookie with a little water and attach the sugarpaste circles in place, pressing them down lightly to secure.

4 Using the blade of a palette knife, gently mark lines vertically and then horizontally across each cookie, spacing the lines approximately 1cm (⅜in) apart.

5 With a paintbrush, apply a dot of water to each point where the lines intersect and add a silver dragee to each dot. Press each dragee down lightly with your fingertip to help them stay in place.

6 Cut out 12 large blossoms from the pale purple sugarpaste and 12 from the darker purple sugarpaste. Place one pale blossom on top of a darker one with the petals slightly offset. Add a silver dragee to the centre of each flower. Make 24 small double blossoms in the same way.

7 Secure one large and two small double blossoms to each cookie with a little water.

Loveheart fountain

MAKING A WIRED CAKE-TOPPER

A mini-cake is brought to life with a dramatic yet super-easy fountain of wired hearts. See what ribbons you've got in your box and adjust the colour scheme to match.

1 Brush the cake card with a little water. Roll out the white sugarpaste to a 3mm (⅛in) thickness. Cut out a 10cm (4in) circle and place onto the cake card to cover it. Neaten around the edges with your fingertips and polish the surface with an icing smoother (see Covering a board with sugarpaste).

2 Roll out some more white sugarpaste, this time to a 5mm (³⁄₁₆in) thickness. Cover

the mini-cake, trimming the excess neatly and polishing with an icing smoother (see Covering a mini-cake).

3 Place the covered mini-cake in the centre of the covered cake card, securing with a dab of buttercream or royal icing. Set aside to let the sugarpaste dry.

4 Trim the bottom of the cake with the purple and pink ribbons, securing at the back of the cake with pearl-headed pins.

Get it together...

- 6.5cm (2½in) round mini-cake, prepared for covering
- 10cm (4in) round cake card
- Sugarpaste: white, purple and hot pink
- Cutters: 10cm (4in) round, mini heart cutters set (PME)
- Buttercream or royal icing
- Posy pick
- Seven gold florists' wires
- Ribbon: purple 2cm (¾in) thick, hot pink 5mm (⅛in) thick
- Pearl-headed pins
- Basic equipment (see Equipment)

TIP
When making cake toppers, push the posy pick into a piece of polystyrene or a potato to keep it steady and upright while you're working on it.

5 Roll out the hot-pink sugarpaste to a 3mm (⅛in) thickness and cut out 17 of the larger hearts. Set eight aside and use the remaining nine around the cake positioning them approximately 1cm (⅜in) apart, 3mm (⅛in) above the ribbon, securing in place with a dab of water.

6 Roll out the purple sugarpaste as before and cut out nine mini hearts and four large hearts. Set the large hearts aside and attach the mini hearts between the hot-pink hearts around the cake with a little water.

7 Take six gold florists' wires and cut each in half. Gather the wires together evenly and wind the seventh piece of wire around the base of the wires to secure them together tightly (see Making a wired cake topper).

8 Fit the wire bunch into a posy pick then curve the wires into position running the wire through your fingertips in the same way as you would curl a ribbon over scissors.

9 Gently push the large purple and hot-pink hearts onto each wire in turn, squeezing with your fingers to secure.

10 Roll a small ball of purple and a small ball of hot-pink sugarpaste and flatten them gently with your hand to create two fat circles. Stack the circles in the centre of the top of the mini-cake and push the posy pick through the centre and down into the cake.

TIP
The number of wires you use for the fountain is up to you – try using more or fewer, you could even try having some shorter lengths and some longer ones.

"When time is short and you haven't been able to let your cake card dry out, place the mini-cake on a chopping board to decorate it, then lift it carefully onto the covered card when done. This will stop you making marks in the wet sugarpaste."

Strawberry fields

CREATING STYLIZED FRUITS

These cute cookies put your heart cutters to good use – they would be perfect for a summer tea party or just to delight the children.

Get it together...

- 12 large and 12 small heart cookies
- Sugarpaste: red, white and green
- Cutters: large and small heart cookie, small square
- Gold sugar dragees
- Basic equipment (see Equipment)

1 Take a small ball of red sugarpaste and knead into the white sugarpaste to create a pink blush colour.

2 Roll out the red sugarpaste to a 3mm (⅛in) thickness. Cut out six large hearts using the large heart cookie cutter and six small hearts using the small heart cookie cutter. Repeat using the pink blush sugarpaste.

3 Brush the top of each cookie with a little water and attach the sugarpaste hearts in place, pressing down lightly to secure.

4 Roll out the green sugarpaste to a 2mm (⅙in). Using the heart cutters again, cut out 24 strawberry hulls (12 large, 12 small) using the top part of the cutters only.

5 Trim down the cut outs and take out the 'V' shapes using the corner of a small square cutter. Secure in place on the strawberries with a dab of water.

6 Shape 24 stalks from the green sugarpaste and fix in place with water.

7 Using the end of your paintbrush, make small indentations for the seeds. Apply a dot of water to each indentation and fill with a gold dragee. Press each dragee down lightly with your fingertip to help them stay in place.

TIP
Rub over the top of the sugarpaste hearts with an icing smoother to remove any finger marks once in place.

Blue blooms

MAKING RUFFLE FLOWERS

These pretty cupcakes have a great wow factor with only a tiny bit of effort. This design would also work on cookies, and in any number of colours.

Get it together...

- Six cupcakes baked in turquoise-blue paper cases
- Buttercream
- Sugarpaste: blue and white
- Round cutters: same size as cupcake tops and 2.5cm (1in)
- Large daisy or blossom cutter
- Blue sugar pearls
- Basic equipment (see Equipment)

TIP
Dust your work surface lightly with icing (confectioners') sugar to stop the sugarpaste sticking.

1 Trim the domes from the tops of your cupcakes and spread a thin layer of buttercream on the top.

2 Roll out the blue sugarpaste to a 3mm (⅛in) thickness. Using a round cutter the same size as the top of your cupcakes, cut out six circles and attach in place on the tops of the cupcakes.

3 Cut out six 2.5cm (1in) circles from the rolled-out blue sugarpaste for the ruffle flowers. Fold each circle roughly in half and then in half again, letting the edges gather together in ruffles. Set to one side.

4 Roll out the white sugarpaste to a 3mm (⅛in) thickness and cut out six daisies or blossoms, depending on the kind of cutter you have.

5 Place the cut-out daisies or blossoms centrally on top of the covered cupcakes, securing in place with a little water.

6 Add a blue ruffle flower to the centre of each cake, again with a dab of water to secure.

7 Place a blue sugar pearl in the centre of each ruffle flower and between each of the white daisy or blossom petals.

Rosebud romance

ROLLING SIMPLE ROSES

This is such a quick cake to put together, no specialist equipment is needed but it has maximum impact! Try different shades for different effects – red for love or purple for passion!

Get it together...

- 20cm (8in) round cake, prepared for covering
- 25cm (10in) round cake board
- Sugarpaste: white, blue and green
- 5cm (2in) wide pale blue ribbon
- Pearl-headed pin
- Edible sparkle lustre dust (optional)
- Basic equipment (see Equipment)

1 Level and prepare the cake for covering (see Levelling and filling a sponge cake). Once chilled, roll out the white sugarpaste to a 5mm (³⁄₁₆in) thickness and use to cover the cake. Trim the excess neatly and polish with an icing smoother (see Covering a cake with sugarpaste).

2 Measure the ribbon and cut to size remembering to leave extra for the tail. Cut a 'V' in the ribbon end and secure using a pearl-headed pin with the tail facing the front.

3 For the first flower, take a ball of blue sugarpaste approximately 7cm (2¾in) in diameter and shape by hand into a rough sausage shape.

TIP
If you don't have an icing smoother, use your hands to smooth and polish the icing. A small ball of sugarpaste wrapped tightly in cling film (plastic wrap) can be rubbed over to smooth out any final bumps.

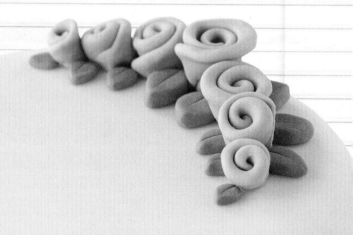

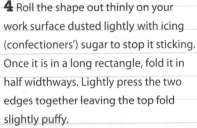

"Don't worry if you don't have a cake board – decorate the cake onto a pretty plate instead. You don't need special brushes either – a clean, dry make-up powder brush is the ideal tool for adding lustre dust."

4 Roll the shape out thinly on your work surface dusted lightly with icing (confectioners') sugar to stop it sticking. Once it is in a long rectangle, fold it in half widthways. Lightly press the two edges together leaving the top fold slightly puffy.

5 Still on the work surface, start to roll the flower up from one end. Once the roll is started, lift it up and hold it with your hands as you continue to roll up the flower (see Making a rolled rose). Pinch off the excess sugarpaste from the base of the flower and set it aside.

6 Repeat the process making seven flowers in total in graduating sizes. Secure the flowers in place on top of the cake using a dab of water.

7 For the leaves, roll small balls of green sugarpaste and flatten with your finger. Pinch the ends of each flattened ball to create the points of the leaf. Mark a central vein down the leaf with the back of a knife. You will need 14 leaves in total, again in graduating sizes.

8 Place a sugarpaste leaf between each of the flowers on both sides, securing with a dab of water. If desired, dust the cake with sparkle lustre dust for bit of extra shimmer!

Buttercup bites

INLAYING A FLORAL PATTERN

These cute cupcakes feature a sugarpaste covering that overhangs the edge of the cupcake case to create a pretty and novel effect.

Get it together...

- Six cupcakes baked in silver foil liners
- Sugarpaste: white, bright yellow and golden yellow
- Cutters: medium and small blossom, 8cm (3in) fluted circle
- Buttercream
- Basic equipment (see Equipment)

"Ensure that your base sheet of sugarpaste is thick enough to begin with. The rolling required to inlay the coloured blossoms means it will end up much thinner than you started with."

1 Roll out the bright yellow and golden yellow sugarpaste to a 2mm (⅟₁₆in) thickness and cut out a variety of blossoms in each colour.

2 Roll out the white sugarpaste to a 5mm (³⁄₁₆in) thickness to form a large rectangle. Take the cut-out blossoms and randomly place onto the white sugarpaste to create a sheet of floral-patterned paste.

3 Roll gently over the sheet with your rolling pin to thin the paste to 3mm (⅛in) and to inlay and seal the yellow blossoms into the white sugarpaste.

4 Coat the tops of the cupcakes with a layer of buttercream.

5 Cut out six fluted circles from the patterned sugarpaste and place on top of each cupcake with the edge of the circle evenly overhanging the cupcake case.

TIP

Any variety of colour combinations and shapes can be used to form a sheet of sugarpaste to work with for lots of different projects – try stars, swirls and butterflies.

Bijoux birthday

MODELLING A MINIATURE CAKE

A mini birthday cake sitting on a beautifully decorated mini-cake looks ever so cute ... who could resist this? Break down the individual modelled parts and it's a doddle too!

Get it together...

- 6.5cm (2½in) round mini-cake, prepared for covering
- 15cm (6in) round cake card
- Sugarpaste: lime green, white, light brown and red
- Buttercream
- Coloured sugar sprinkles: stars and small balls
- Basic equipment (see Equipment)

1 Roll out the white sugarpaste to a 3mm (⅛in) thickness and use to cover the cake card (see Covering a board with sugarpaste).

2 Roll out the lime green sugarpaste to a 5mm (³⁄₁₆in) thickness and use to cover the mini-cake (see Covering a mini-cake).

3 Place the covered mini-cake in the centre of the covered cake card, securing with a dab of buttercream. Set aside to let the sugarpaste dry.

4 Roll two balls of light brown sugarpaste around 3cm (1⅛in) in diameter. Flatten each ball into a disc. Spend time shaping each so that they are roughly the same shape and thickness.

5 Flatten a ball of red sugarpaste into a thin disc to create the jam filling. Indent the edges of the 'jam' circle slightly using the end of a paintbrush.

6 Repeat for the icing on top of the cake using white sugarpaste, making the disc slightly smaller than the top of the cake. Stack the pieces together to form the

cake. Moisten the icing of the miniature cake with a tiny bit of water and sprinkle lightly with the ball sprinkles.

7 To create the candle, roll a tiny sausage of lime green sugarpaste and flatten each end slightly. Take a yellow star from the sprinkles, insert one point of the star into the end of the candle and position in place on top of the miniature cake, securing with a dab of water.

8 To create the candle, roll a tiny sausage of lime green sugarpaste and flatten each end slightly. Take a yellow star from the sprinkles, insert one point of the star into the end of the candle and position in place on top of the miniature cake, securing with a dab of water.

9 Decorate the sides of the cake using white star sprinkles, applying a dab of water to the back of each star before pressing lightly into place. Roll a long sausage of lime green sugarpaste and wrap around the base of the cake, trimming neatly at the back.

TIP
If you're struggling to get the candle to keep its shape, form it around a piece of dried spaghetti, but do make sure you warn whoever will be eating it!

Swirling stars

CREATING A DECKLE EDGE

A fluted cutter is used in this design to give a textured edge to the swirls. Stars are a great motif that can be used in a myriad of colours for any number of different occasions.

Get it together...

- Six cupcakes baked in purple paper cases
- Buttercream
- Sugarpaste: white and mid-purple
- Cutters: round (same size as cupcake tops), large and small stars, graduated fluted round cutters
- Edible silver glitter
- Basic equipment (see Equipment)

TIP

Let the large stars dry out slightly before adding them to the cupcakes so that you can position them overlapping the edge of each cupcake without them drooping.

1 Trim the domes from the tops of your cupcakes if necessary and spread a thin layer of buttercream on the top.

2 Roll out the white sugarpaste to a 3mm (⅛in) thickness. Using a round cutter the same size as the top of your cakes, cut out six circles and attach in place on the tops of the cupcakes.

3 Roll out the purple sugarpaste to a 3mm (⅛in) thickness. Using a fluted cutter, cut out six circles slightly smaller than the size of the cupcake tops.

4 Take the next smallest fluted cutter from the set and cut out the centres of the purple circles. Discard the centres. Cut each circle and open out the thin fluted pieces.

5 Brush the back of each piece with a little water and place in the shape of a swirl on top of each cupcake.

6 Cut out six large white stars and 12 small purple stars and brush the backs with a little water. Position the large star towards the left-hand side of the cupcake. Place one small purple star on top of the larger white star and one in the centre of the swirl.

7 Sprinkle with a little edible glitter – because they're worth it!

Chocolate starburst

CREATING STARBURST FLOWERS

Using chocolate sugarpaste for this mini-cake takes out the laborious task of colouring sugarpaste a deep brown – all the work is done for you!

Get it together...

- 6.5cm (2½in) round mini-cake, prepared for covering
- 10cm (4in) round cake card
- Sugarpaste: chocolate and turquoise
- Buttercream
- Round cutters: 2cm (¾in), 3cm (1in), 4cm (1½in) and 10cm (4in)
- Basic equipment (see Equipment)

1 Roll out the chocolate sugarpaste to a 3mm (⅛in) thickness. Cut out a 10cm (4in) circle and use to cover the cake card (see Covering a board with sugarpaste).

2 Roll out some more chocolate sugarpaste to a 5mm (³⁄₁₆in) thickness. Cover the mini-cake, trimming the excess neatly and polishing with an icing smoother (see Covering a mini-cake).

3 Place the covered mini-cake in the centre of the covered cake card, securing with a dab of buttercream. Set aside to let the sugarpaste dry.

4 Gather the trimmings of the chocolate sugarpaste and roll out to a 3mm (⅛in) thickness. Cut out four 4cm (1½in) circles and four 2cm (¾in) circles. Using the corresponding sized cutter, cut the edges from the circle, creating four petals from each. Repeat with the turquoise sugarpaste creating four 3cm (1in) circles and dividing each into four petals.

5 Begin to form the three starburst flowers on the cake using the largest chocolate petals first. Each flower has five petals. Secure each in place with a little water applied to the back of the petal. Build up the flower using the turquoise petals then the small chocolate petals.

6 Roll a small ball of turquoise sugarpaste for the centres of the flowers and secure in place with a dab of water.

7 Finish the cake by rolling a thin sausage of turquoise sugarpaste between an icing smoother and your work surface to get a good length and an even width. Place the sausage around the base of the cake and trim neatly at the back.

TIP

When working with dark-coloured sugarpaste such as chocolate, avoid getting icing (confectioners') sugar on the surface as it can mark the sugarpaste and be difficult to get off.

Marble bow

CREATING A MARBLED EFFECT

The gorgeous rippling colours in this classic cake design look hard to achieve but it couldn't be simpler – just mix them up and roll!

Get it together...

- 20cm (8in) round cake, prepared for covering
- 25cm (10in) round cake board
- Buttercream
- Sugarpaste: purple, pink and pale blue
- Pizza cutter
- Serrated steak knife
- 12mm (½in) wide purple ribbon
- Pearl-headed pins
- Basic equipment (see Equipment)

1 Level and prepare the cake for covering (see Levelling and filling a sponge cake). Once chilled, set the cake centrally onto the cake board, securing with a dab of buttercream.

2 Roll each of the sugarpaste colours into long, thick sausages. Position the rolls side by side and squeeze together gently. Fold the long sausage in half and then in half again. Roll out this ball of striped sugarpaste to a 5mm (³⁄₁₆in) thickness and use to cover the cake. The marbled effect is created as you roll out the paste. Trim the excess neatly and polish with an icing smoother (see Covering a cake with sugarpaste).

3 Gather the trimmings together and knead until a smooth even colour is achieved. Form a thick sausage and roll out into a long, thin strip 4mm (⅛in) thick. Using a pizza cutter, cut the strip into four 4cm (1½in) wide strips, each 20cm (8in) long.

4 Using a serrated steak knife, gently imprint the stitching pattern on each edge of the strips, approximately 5mm (³⁄₁₆in) away from the edges.

5 Apply a little water to the cake and secure each strip in place. Trim any excess off the strips in the centre.

6 To create the bow, cut another strip of sugarpaste, this time 24cm (9½in)

long and 8cm (3in) wide, and mark with stitching lines as before. Turn the strip over so the right side is facing the work surface. Fold in each end to the middle and pinch the bow in the centre gently.

7 For the centre of the bow, take a 2.5cm (1in) strip, mark with stitching lines and wrap the ends underneath the back of the bow. Position the bow in place in the centre of the cake.

8 Trim the base of the cake and the edge of the board with purple ribbon, securing at the back with pearl-headed pins.

"Marbling sugarpaste works with all sorts of coordinating colours and is a great way of using up excess pieces left over from other projects. It means you can get a great cake with the minimum of fuss!"

Polka-dot candles

INCOPORATING CANDLEHOLDERS
INTO A DESIGN

Often when decorating cakes we forget to leave space in the design for candles. Not here – this cake is designed with the birthday candles in mind!

Get it together...

- 20cm (8in) round cake, prepared for covering
- 30cm (12in) round cake board
- Eight 10cm (4in) celebration candles
- Buttercream
- Sugarpaste: pink and white
- Round cutters: straight-edged 2.5cm (1in), fluted 3.5cm (1½in)
- 12mm (½in) wide pale pink ribbon
- Pearl-headed pins
- Basic equipment (see Equipment)

1 Level and prepare the cake for covering (see Levelling and filling a sponge cake). Once chilled, set the cake centrally onto the cake board, securing with a dab of buttercream.

2 Roll out the pale pink sugarpaste to a 5mm (³⁄₁₆in) thickness and use to cover the cake. Trim the excess neatly and polish with an icing smoother (see Covering a cake with sugarpaste).

3 Roll out the white sugarpaste to a 3mm (⅛in) thickness. Using the straight-edged cutter, cut out 20 circles. Using the fluted cutter, cut out eight fluted circles. Cut out the centres of the fluted circles using the straight-edged cutter and set these to one side.

4 Attach the straight-edged white circles to the cake with a little water in a polka dot pattern across the top and around the sides of the cake.

5 Roll eight 4cm (1½in) balls of pale pink sugarpaste and flatten slightly. Take one candle at a time and press the base into the flattened ball to create the candleholder.

6 Drop one of the fluted circles down over the candle so that it sits on the pink sugarpaste holder.

"A water brush will save you time when applying dabs of water, they can be picked up fairly cheaply in most arts and craft stores."

7 Position each of the candles and their holders onto the cake board, spaced evenly around the cake. A little dab of water on the base of each holder will secure it in place.

8 Roll 16 pink and 16 white 1.5cm (½in) diameter balls in the palms of your hands. Position the pink and white balls alternately between each candleholder using a dab of water on the base to secure them.

9 Trim the edge of the board with pale pink ribbon, securing at the back with a pearl-headed pin.

Half-Day
Delights

Regal roses

PIPING ROYAL ICING ROSES

The thought of entirely piping the decoration onto a cake may well send you into a panic – fear not, these stylized piped swirl roses are super easy.

Get it together...

- 20cm (8in) square cake, prepared for covering
- 30cm (12in) square cake board
- Sugarpaste: purple
- Royal icing: dark purple and leaf green
- Piping (pastry) bags and no. 2, no. 8 and leaf (no. 2B) nozzles (tips)
- 12mm (½in) wide purple ribbon
- Pearl-headed pins
- Basic equipment (see Equipment)

1 Roll out the purple sugarpaste to a 3mm (⅛in) thickness and use to cover the cake board (see Covering a board with sugarpaste). Lightly spraying the board with a mist from a water spray will help the sugarpaste to stick.

2 Roll out more of the purple sugarpaste to a 5mm (³⁄₁₆in) thickness and cover the cake. Trim the excess neatly and polish with an icing smoother (see Covering a cake with sugarpaste). Set both the board and the cake to one side to allow the sugarpaste to begin to dry.

3 Split a batch of royal icing into two. Colour one portion dark purple and the other leaf green using edible gel paste colours (see Colouring).

4 Position the cake in the centre of the covered board, securing with a dab of royal icing.

5 Using a piping (pastry) bag fitted with a no. 8 nozzle (tip), pipe a purple royal icing shell border around the base of the cake (see Piping a shell border).

6 Mark positioning pinpricks on the top of the cake – these will guide you when piping each rose or cluster. Using a piping (pastry) bag fitted with a no. 2 nozzle

(tip), pipe swirls of purple royal icing onto each marked position to create the roses. For the clusters of flowers, try to pipe them so that they just touch each other. If your piped swirls have a peaked end dab them down with a damp paintbrush.

> **TIP**
> Practise piping on a sheet of greaseproof (wax) paper before piping onto the cake. This will give you a good feel for the action and pressure needed to create the swirls.

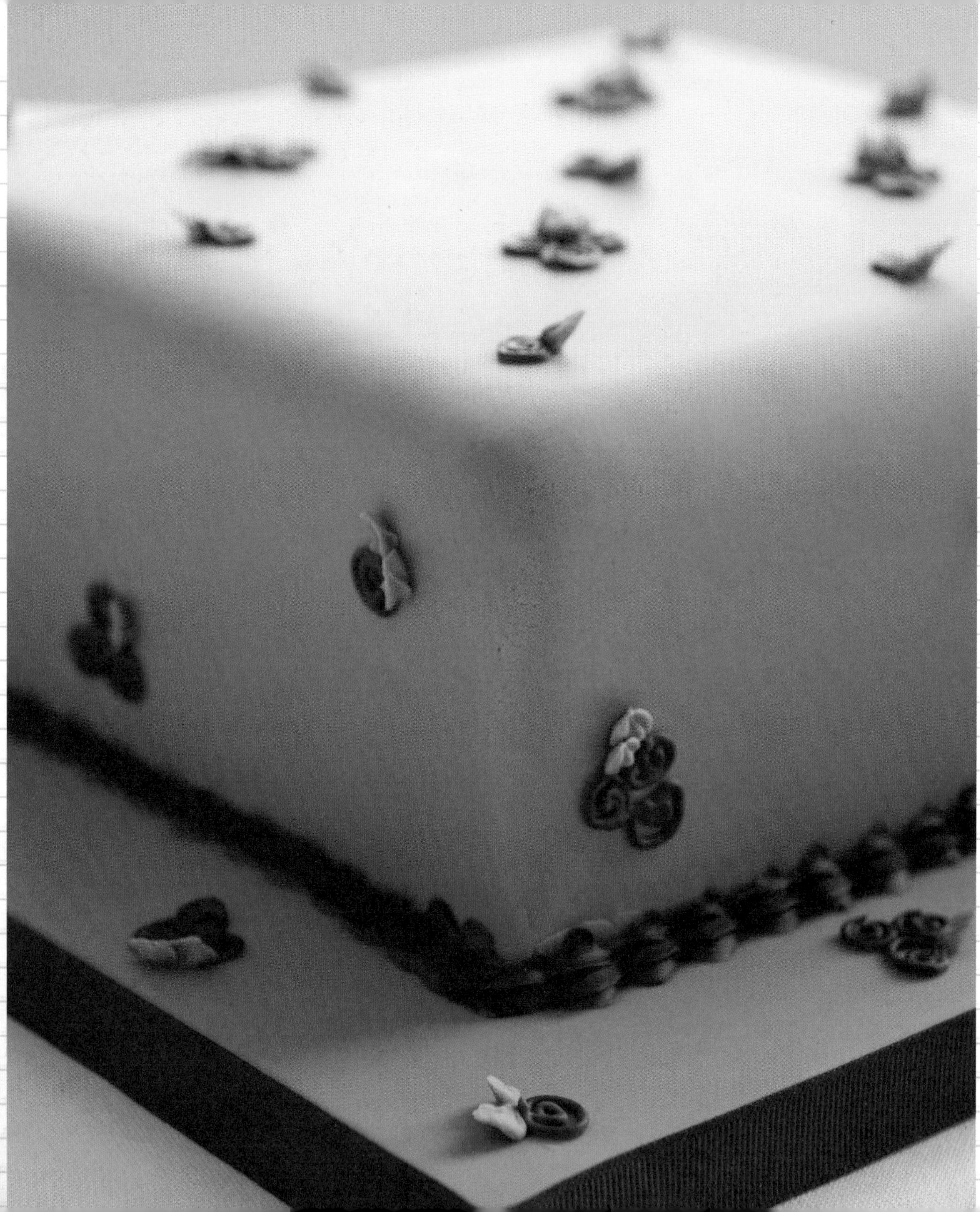

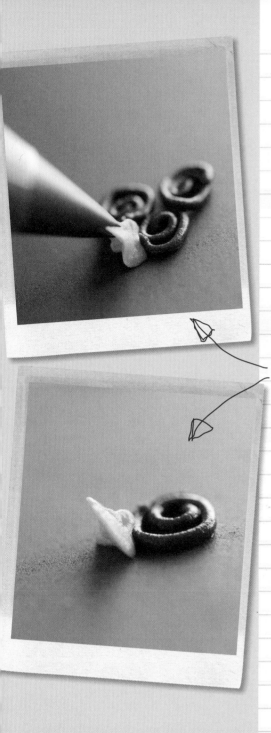

7 Once the top has been piped, begin piping on each side of the cake. Piping vertically will need a slightly different technique so tape a piece of greaseproof (wax) paper to the side of a box for a quick practice run! Add swirl roses around the cake board.

8 Take the green royal icing and place in a piping (pastry) bag fitted with a leaf nozzle (tip) (no. 2B). Begin piping the leaf right next to the purple swirl. Keep the nozzle (tip) in the same position while applying pressure to the bag, once the base of the leaf is the correct size release the pressure completely and then pull away. This will create the pointed tip of the leaf. Pipe a leaf next to each swirl flower across the cake and board.

9 Finish by trimming the board with purple ribbon, securing at the back with a pearl-headed pin.

"If you are using disposable bags, the quickest thing to do is to cut the no. 8 nozzle (tip) from the bag and drop the whole lot into a new bag fitted with the no. 2 nozzle (tip)."

TIP

If you don't have a leaf nozzle (tip) just cut a small inverted 'V' from the end of a disposable piping (pastry) bag. This will give you the same effect.

Romantic ruffles

CREATING LARGE-SCALE RUFFLES

Bring a bit of frilly frou-frou to your day! Girly and beautifully decadent, this mini-cake will be adored by everyone.

Get it together...

- 6.5cm (2½in) round mini-cake, prepared for covering
- 10cm (4in) round cake card
- Sugarpaste: white and pale pink
- Cutters: 10cm (4in) and 5cm (2in) round
- Empty egg box
- Royal icing
- Piping (pastry) bag and no. 2 nozzle (tube)
- Silver sugar dragees – hearts and balls
- Basic equipment (see Equipment)

TIP

If the join between the cake and the board is a bit untidy, use a bigger nozzle (tip) (such as a no.43) to pipe the snail trail, as this will help disguise it.

1 Brush the cake card with a little water. Roll out the white sugarpaste to a 3mm (⅛in) thickness. Cut out a 10cm (4in) circle and place onto the cake card to cover it. Neaten around the edges with your fingertips and polish the surface with an icing smoother (see Covering a board with sugarpaste).

2 Roll out some more white sugarpaste, this time to a 5mm (³⁄₁₆in) thickness. Cover the mini-cake, trimming the excess neatly and polishing with an icing smoother (see Covering a mini-cake).

3 Place the covered mini-cake in the centre of the covered cake card, securing with a dab of royal icing. Set aside to let the sugarpaste dry.

4 Roll out the pale pink sugarpaste to a 3mm (⅛in) thickness and cut out eight 5cm (2in) circles. With the first circle create a ruffle, folding the circle roughly in half and then in half again, letting the edges gather together in ruffles.

5 Pinch the base slightly to form a point. Place in the recess of an empty egg box to help the ruffle hold its shape. Repeat with the remaining circles. Allow to dry out for an hour so that they are easier to handle without breaking.

6 Meanwhile, using the royal icing, pipe a snail trail (see Piping a snail trail) around the base of the cake, securing it to the board. At the base of the cake make four pinpricks equally spaced apart, each one-quarter of the way around the circumference of the cake.

7 Pipe a dot of royal icing at each mark and secure a silver heart dragee in place. With further dots of royal icing, secure three silver ball dragees above each heart.

8 Mark three pinpricks equally spaced apart between each silver heart dragee. Again, with dots of royal icing apply three silver ball dragees vertically at each pinprick.

9 Once your ruffles have firmed up, pipe a layer of royal icing on top of the mini-cake. Begin sticking six pink ruffles in place around the edge and then finally add two in the centre.

Buttoned up

EMBOSSING SUGAR BUTTONS

The beautiful patterns on the button embellishments on these cupcakes are created by embossing the paste. The peachy petals create the perfect foil.

Get it together...

- Six cupcakes baked in orange gingham paper cases
- Buttercream
- Sugarpaste: orange, white and red
- Round cutters: 2.5cm (1in) and 4cm (1½in)
- Edible gold lustre dust
- Variety of objects for embossing e.g. texture mat, lace or buttons
- Pencil
- Basic equipment (see Equipment)

1 Begin by making the buttons for the centres of the flowers. Roll out the red sugarpaste to a 3mm (⅛in) thickness and emboss the surface using a piece of lace, the face of a pretty button or a texture mat (see Embossing). Make sure the imprint is deep enough. Cut out six 2.5cm (1in) circles.

2 Indent the centre of each circle with the flat end of a pencil. Using the end of a paintbrush, punch two holes through the sugarpaste to create the centre of each button. Set the buttons to one side to firm up.

3 Once the buttons have set, dust each one with a little gold lustre dust using a soft brush.

4 Roll the white and orange sugarpastes into long, thick sausages. Position the rolls side by side and squeeze together gently. Fold the long sausage in half and then in half again. Roll out this ball of striped sugarpaste to a 3mm (⅛in) thickness. The marbling effect is created as you roll out the paste.

5 Using the 4cm (1½in) cutter, cut out 24 circles. Take each one and pinch together across the circle, approximately one-third of the way in from the edge, to create a petal. Repeat with the remaining circles until you have created all 24 petals.

6 Cover each cupcake with a layer of buttercream. Position four petals on the top of each cupcake. Apply a dab of water to the back of a button and position centrally onto the petals.

Ice lollies

MAKING COOKIES ON STICKS

Conjure up childhood memories or delight today's kids with these fantastic facsimile ice lollies, which won't melt even on the hottest of days!

Get it together...

- Cookie dough (see Vanilla sugar cookies), rolled out and chilled
- Six wooden lollipop sticks
- Sugarpaste: pink, white, brown, red, orange and yellow
- Coloured sugar sprinkles
- Pizza cutter
- Basic equipment (see Equipment)

1 Cut a long strip of cookie dough approximately 7cm (2¾in) wide using a pizza cutter. Cut into six individual rectangular cookies, each 4.5cm (1¾in) wide. Using a sharp knife, round the corners of the top edge. Shape six further cookies into rectangles and then with a sharp knife cut off the sides to create the triangular lolly shapes.

2 Transfer the cookies onto a baking tray lined with greaseproof (wax) paper. Once the cookies have softened slightly, take the wooden lollipop sticks and cut each in half. Insert one half into the base of each cookie, taking care not to split the dough.

3 Place the baking tray in the fridge and chill for 15 minutes until firm. Bake as per the recipe instructions (see Vanilla sugar cookies]) and allow to cool.

4 Roll out the pink, white and brown sugarpaste into long sausages and lay on the work surface in the correct colour order side by side. Squeeze together gently to join. Roll out lengthways to form a sheet of striped sugarpaste approximately 3mm (⅛in) thick.

5 For the 'FAB' lollies, cut out six rectangles of the striped sugarpaste to fit each of the rectangular cookies and secure using a little water. Trim the rounded corners.

6 Place the coloured sugar sprinkles into a small bowl, paint the brown sugarpaste section lightly with water and dip into the sprinkles to coat.

7 For the 'Rocket' lollies, repeat the sausage method for the red, orange and yellow sugarpaste and cut out shapes to cover the top of the triangular cookies, again securing in place with a little water.

8 Using a wooden lollipop stick, mark an indent on either side to create the fins of the rocket.

"If these cookies are a real hit with the kids, make up a double batch and freeze the dough ready rolled and cut into shape to save time next time you make them."

TIP

If the cookies spread too much in the oven, take a sharp knife and re-trim while they are still warm.

Spring has sprung

COMBINING PIPING WITH CUT OUTS

This project reminds me very much of scrapbooking – cut out plenty of the elements and then play around as if creating a collage.

Get it together...

- 25cm (10in) round cake, prepared for covering
- 32cm (13in) round cake board
- Sugarpaste: white, dark pink and pale pink
- Cutters: small butterfly, small and extra-small blossom
- Empty egg box
- Royal icing: pink and white
- Piping (pastry) bags and no. 2 and no. 0 (or no. 1) nozzles (tips)
- Pink and pearl sugar dragees, medium and tiny
- Edible pink lustre dust
- Ribbon: pale pink 70mm (2¾in) wide, pale pink 12mm (½in) wide
- Pearl-headed pins
- Basic equipment (see Equipment)

1 Roll out the white sugarpaste to a 3mm (⅛in) thickness and use to cover the cake board (see Covering a board with sugarpaste). Lightly spraying the board with a mist from a water spray will help the sugarpaste to stick.

2 Roll out more of the white sugarpaste to a 5mm (³⁄₁₆in) thickness and cover the cake. Trim the excess neatly and polish with an icing smoother (see Covering a cake with sugarpaste). Set both the board and the cake to one side to allow the sugarpaste to begin to dry.

3 Roll out a little more white sugarpaste to a 3mm (⅛in) thickness and cut out six small butterflies. Place the butterflies into the recesses of an empty egg box to curl the wings slightly and allow to dry. Dusting the egg box with a little icing (confectioners') sugar will prevent them from sticking.

4 Thinly roll out a little pale and dark pink sugarpaste. Stamp out a good amount of small and extra-small blossom shapes in both colours. If using a plunger cutter, stamp out the blossom and with it still in the cutter, position the back of the blossom on your fingertip dusted lightly with icing (confectioners') sugar. Press down the plunger to shape the blossom against your finger then set down on your work surface.

TIP
Using the plunger to shape the blossom on your finger rather than doing it on the work surface creates a much nicer shape of blossom.

"Any excess blossoms not used for this project can be kept in a small jar once they have dried out and used on other projects at a later date."

5 Using a piece of greaseproof (wax) paper, trace the template for the piped swirls outline (see Templates). Place the template gently onto the top of the covered cake and softly trace the outline with the end of a paintbrush to indent the pattern onto the icing. You can then use this as a guide when piping.

6 Fill a piping (pastry) bag fitted with a no. 2 nozzle (tip) with pink royal icing. Pipe a small section of the swirls at a time. If the piping has little peaks, dab them down using a damp paintbrush. When piping, work from one side of the cake to the other, taking care not to smudge it with your hand as you continue. Pipe pink dots to the end of the swirls as shown on the template.

"Use disposable piping bags to save time, and to save on the washing up too!"

7 Take the white royal icing and fill a piping (pastry) bag fitted with a no. 0 or no. 1 nozzle (tip). Pipe five small dots of icing onto each of the four positions marked on the template and place two pink, one pearl and two tiny pearl dragees onto the dots as shown in the photo.

8 Apply a dot of icing at each of the three pink piped intersections and secure a small blossom in place. Pipe a dot to create the centre of each blossom.

9 Continue to decorate the cake with the blossoms, securing each and creating the centres with white royal icing. Position them in a variety of clusters using single blossoms, pairs and threes.

10 Dust the centres of the butterflies with a little pink lustre dust. Secure each butterfly onto the cake using a dab of white royal icing. Pipe a pink snail trail (see Piping a snail trail) down the centre of each butterfly to create the body.

TIP

Any wobbly sections or breaks in your piping can be covered using a blossom or a butterfly.

11 Position the cake centrally onto the cake board securing with a little royal icing. Trim the cake using the wide pink ribbon, securing at the back of the cake with two pearl-headed pins. The ribbon should sit flush with the cake board.

12 Trim the edge of the board with narrow pink ribbon, securing at the back with a pearl-headed pin.

13 Decorate the cake board using the remaining pink blossoms and butterflies.

Blossoming all over

DENSELY DECORATING A MINI-CAKE

A beautiful mini-cake bursting with beautiful colours is sure to bring a smile to anyone's face.

Get it together...

- 6.5cm (2½in) mini-cake, prepared for covering
- 10cm (4in) round cake card
- Sugarpaste: cream, mauve, yellow, pink and deep pink
- Cutters: 10cm (4in) round, small and medium blossoms
- Royal icing
- Piping (pastry) bag and no. 3 nozzle (tip)
- 12mm (½in) wide pale purple ribbon
- Pearl-headed pins
- Basic equipment (see Equipment)

1 Roll out the cream sugarpaste to a 3mm (⅛in) thickness, cut out a 10cm (4in) circle and cover the cake card (see Covering a board with sugarpaste).

2 Cover the mini-cake with more of the cream sugarpaste, this time rolled out to a 5mm (³⁄₁₆in) thickness. Trim off any excess neatly and polish using an icing smoother (see Covering a mini-cake). Set the cake onto the covered board and secure with a little royal icing.

3 Trim the base of the cake with pale purple ribbon, securing at the back of the cake with a pearl-headed pin.

4 Roll out each colour of sugarpaste in turn and cut out two large blossoms and approximately 20 small blossoms from each colour.

> ### TIP
> To pick up and attach each of the blossoms, press the end of a paintbrush lightly into the centre, this will also curve the petals outwards prettily.

5 Using the end of a paintbrush, secure each of the large blossoms around the cake with a dot of royal icing and then begin to fill in the gaps using the small blossoms. Keep the colour order random and take care with the spacing so as not to leave any large gaps. The petals of the blossoms can overlap the ribbon at the base of the cake. Once the sides are fully filled, apply the blossoms to the top of the cake.

6 Pipe a dot of royal icing into the centre of each blossom until all the flowers have white centres.

"This is a great way of using up small balls of sugarpaste left over from other projects that really don't seem big enough to do anything with. Have a play with your leftovers and see what colour scheme you can come up with!"

Floral flourish

TEXTURING AND LAYERING FLOWERS

This project takes a little more planning and patience in forming the flowers but it is definitely worth it for stunning results.

Get it together...

- Six cupcakes baked in bright pink paper cases
- Buttercream
- Sugarpaste: white and pale pink
- Cutters: large and small blossom cutter, round (same size as cupcake tops)
- Royal icing: bright pink
- Piping (pastry) bag and no. 2 nozzle (tip)
- Basic equipment (see Equipment)

TIP

If your dots of royal icing have peaks on them, gently press them down with a slightly damp paintbrush for a professional rounded finish.

1 Begin by starting work on the flowers. Roll out the white sugarpaste to a 2mm (1/16in) thickness. Stamp out 12 large and 12 small blossoms.

2 With a sharp knife, cut into each petal of the blossoms, separating them into four or five fronds each.

3 Using a dab of water, secure the blossoms together in pairs, placing them with the petals slightly offset.

4 Set the six large and six small blossoms to one side and allow to firm up slightly.

5 Trim the domes from the tops of your cupcakes and spread a thin layer of buttercream on the top.

6 Roll out the pale pink sugarpaste to a 3mm (1/8in) thickness. Using a round cutter the same size as the top of your cupcakes, cut out six circles and attach in place on the tops of the cupcakes.

7 Add the royal icing to a piping (pastry) bag fitted with a no. 2 nozzle (tip). Pipe a dot of royal icing in the centre of the top of the cupcake and place the large flower in place.

8 In the centre of the flower pipe another dot of royal icing and position the small flower in the centre.

9 Pipe eight small dots of royal icing to create the centre of the flower.

10 Pipe small bulbs of royal icing around the flower onto the pale pink sugarpaste to create polka dots.

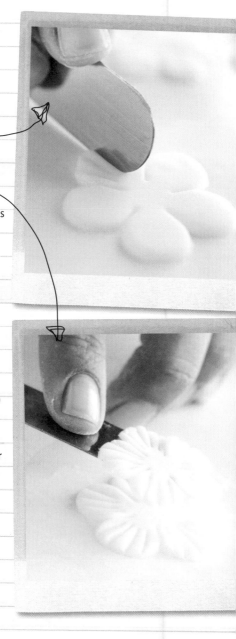

Pretty in pink

BRUSHING ROYAL ICING DESIGNS

Brushed royal icing creates a stunning effect – once you start you won't want to stop. Just let the brush do the work for you!

Get it together...

- 12 round cookies
- Round cutters: straight-edged 5.75cm (2¼in), fluted 6.5cm (2½in)
- Sugarpaste: cream and pink
- Royal icing
- Piping (pastry) bag and no. 2 nozzle (tip)
- Basic equipment (see Equipment)

TIP
Keep dampening your brush as you work – it should remain barely damp throughout. Don't let it dry out!

1 Roll out the cream sugarpaste to a 3mm (⅛in) thickness. Using the fluted cutter, cut out 12 circles.

2 Brush the top of each cookie with a tiny amount of water and attach the fluted sugarpaste circles in place, pressing down lightly to secure.

3 Roll out the pink sugarpaste to a 3mm (⅛in) thickness. Using the straight-edged cutter, cut out 12 circles. Attach each pink circle centrally on the cream fluted circle.

4 Take the medium blossom cutter and press lightly into the centre of each pink circle to create a blossom imprint.

5 Using the small blossom cutter, repeat to mark two small blossoms either side of the medium blossom. These will be your guides when piping.

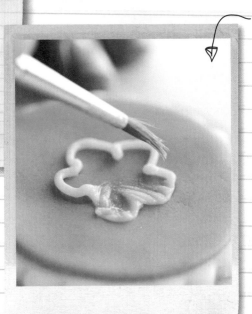

6 Fill a piping (pastry) bag fitted with a no. 2 nozzle (tip) with white royal icing. Working on one cookie at a time, pipe a complete line around the outline of the medium blossom.

7 Take your paintbrush and dip it in water. To remove the excess water, pat the bristles lightly on a piece of kitchen paper. The brush needs to be barely wet.

8 Flatten the line of piped royal icing using the brush, stroking the icing in towards the centre of the blossom. Repeat, working your way around the outer edge of the flower.

9 Pipe five small dots at the tip of each small blossom petal. Use your dampened paintbrush to drag the dots into a petal shape moving towards the centre of each small blossom.

10 Pipe a curved line of four dots from the centre flower to the small blossoms as shown. Pipe six small dots in the middle of the medium blossom to create the centre of the flower.

11 At the top and bottom of each cookie, pipe a small line with two dots at each end. Repeat with your whole batch of cookies and allow the icing to dry.

Weekend
Wonders

Seeing stars

DENSELY DECORATING A TIERED CAKE

This is a grand cake that you just need a bit of time for – nothing tricky for spectacular results! The colour scheme can be changed to suit whoever you're baking for.

Get it together...

- Square cakes: 20cm (8in) and 30cm (12in), both prepared for covering
- 35cm (14in) square cake board
- Square cake cards: 20cm (8in) and 30cm (12in)
- Buttercream
- Four plastic cake dowels
- Royal icing
- Sugarpaste: white and blue
- Star cutters: large, small and tiny
- Silver sugar dragees
- 12mm (½in) wide blue ribbon
- Pearl-headed pins
- Basic equipment (see Equipment)

1 Roll out the white sugarpaste to a 3mm (⅛in) thickness and use to cover the cake board (see Covering a board with sugarpaste). Trim the edges neatly and set aside.

2 Place each cake on the corresponding cake card, securing with a little buttercream, and cover each with white sugarpaste (see Covering a cake with sugarpaste). Allow the boards and cakes to dry out overnight before assembling and decorating.

3 Apply a smear of royal icing to the centre of the covered cake board. Position the larger cake squarely in the centre of the board. Measure and trim the dowels (see Stacking a tiered cake) and push them down firmly into the larger cake.

"If you're new to covering cakes, try using a non-stick mat to roll out your sugarpaste. You will still need a little icing (confectioners') sugar but the mat will really help. Roll out the sugarpaste fairly thickly – about 7mm (¼in). This will help you get a good finish and avoid rips and cracks."

TIP
Edible glue, available from cake decorating suppliers, holds stronger than water. If you're starting to build up a collection of decorating equipment then this is definitely something to have in your box of tricks.

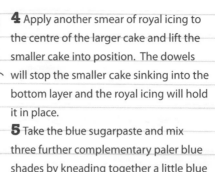

4 Apply another smear of royal icing to the centre of the larger cake and lift the smaller cake into position. The dowels will stop the smaller cake sinking into the bottom layer and the royal icing will hold it in place.

5 Take the blue sugarpaste and mix three further complementary paler blue shades by kneading together a little blue with increasing amounts of white. Roll out a small amount of each colour and cut out a selection of different sized stars in each shade.

6 Starting from the very top centre of the cake, apply a dab of water and fix a star in place. Continue attaching the stars in a random pattern working outwards and downwards evenly around the cake. Apply stars across where the two cakes meet, around the corners and also where there are any flaws in the white sugarpaste.

7 Continue rolling out the sugarpaste and building up the covering of stars until you reach the cake board. Trim any stars as necessary where they meet the board.

8 Cut out some tiny stars in all of the different colours and position them between the larger stars.

9 Apply two or three silver dragees along one of the points on each of the larger stars and some of the smaller ones too. To help them stay put, make gentle indentations with the end of the paintbrush then glue them in place with a dab of water and a quick press of the fingertip. If the sugarpaste stars feel too dry to indent, use the end of the paintbrush in a twisting action gently drilling a little hole – this will stop the paste cracking.

10 Finish by placing a length of ribbon around each tier and the edge of the board, securing with pearl-headed pins.

TIP

Make sure you mix up enough of each colour the first time, as it can be difficult to match the colour if you run out.

Peaches & cream

CREATING A LACE EFFECT WITH CUT OUTS

Cakes don't need to be big and bold to create impact. This stunning little number takes time and patience, but the results are worth the effort.

Get it together...

- 20cm (8in) round cake, prepared for covering
- 25cm (10in) square cake board
- Sugarpaste: peach and cream
- Round cutters: straight-edged 3.5cm (1⅜in), fluted 4.5cm (1¾in), no. 2 piping nozzle (tip)
- 12mm (½in) wide cream ribbon
- Pearl-headed pins
- Basic equipment (see Equipment)

1 Roll out the cream sugarpaste to a 3mm (⅛in) thickness and use to cover the cake board (see Covering a board with sugarpaste). Lightly spraying the board with a mist from a water spray will help the sugarpaste to stick.

2 Roll out the peach sugarpaste to a 5mm (³⁄₁₆in) thickness and cover the cake. Trim the excess neatly and polish with an icing smoother (see Covering a cake with sugarpaste). Set the board and the cake to one side to allow the sugarpaste to begin to dry.

3 Roll out a little cream sugarpaste to a 2–3mm (¹⁄₁₆–⅛in) thickness. To create the shapes for the lace pattern, begin by cutting out circles using the fluted cutter. Cut out the centres with the smaller straight-edged cutter.

"Getting the pieces into position, without losing their shape can be a little tricky. Position them upside down on your fingers and then tip them over into position, or try lifting them with a palette knife and sliding them off onto the cake."

TIP
When working with very thin sugarpaste, instead of dusting your surface with sugar try using a smear of white vegetable fat (shortening).

4 Take one of the discarded inner circles and cut it into sixths using a sharp knife. From each triangle cut three tiny circles using the narrow end of the no. 2 piping nozzle (tip).

5 Cut out small circles using the wide end of the no. 2 piping nozzle (tip) then punch eight small holes around the edge of each with the narrow end.

6 Take each thin fluted circle, gently ease the shape together approximately one-third of the way across the circle to form a closed horseshoe shape and trim the excess using a sharp knife.

7 Once you have made a few of each element, begin securing into place with a dab of water on the back of each piece.

8 Continue creating the elements and expanding the design until the cake is completely covered. There are two strips of lace going across the top of the cake and one curved section on either side.

9 To finish off the edge of each strip of lace, cut several large fluted circles and cut out the inners with a straight-edged cutter leaving a thin fluted circle. Cut open the circles and form into straight lines. Secure in place along each strip of lace on the cake using as many as required and trimming them where the cake meets the board.

10 Trim around the base of the cake and the edge of the board with cream ribbon, securing with pearl-headed pins.

> **TIP**
> When punching out small holes, regularly dip the end of the nozzle (tip) into a little icing (confectioners') sugar to ensure a clean cut.

TIP
The small holes need to be punched out while the sugarpaste is still supple otherwise the edges of the triangles will crack.

Pink whisk

MAKING A STATEMENT PIECE

Inspiration for cakes comes from all sorts of different places, this two-tier lovely is based on the design of my own website – I even have an apron to match!

Get it together...

- Round cakes: 20cm (8in) and 28cm (11in), both prepared for covering
- 33cm (13in) round cake board
- 20cm (8in) round cake card
- Four plastic cake dowels
- Sugarpaste: pale blue, white, pale pink and deep pink
- Round cutters: 2cm (¾in) and 5cm (2in)
- Buttercream or royal icing
- Pizza cutter
- Fluted pastry roller
- 12mm (½in) wide white ribbon
- Pearl-headed pins
- Basic equipment (see Equipment)

1 Roll out the white sugarpaste to a 3mm (⅛in) thickness and use to cover the 33cm (13in) board (see Covering a board with sugarpaste).

2 Set the 20cm (8in) cake on the 20cm (8in) cake card, securing with a little buttercream. Roll out the pale blue sugarpaste to a 5mm (³⁄₁₆in) thickness and use to cover the cake and board together, trimming the excess neatly and polishing with an icing smoother (see Covering a cake with sugarpaste).

3 Roll out the pale pink sugarpaste to a 5mm (³⁄₁₆in) thickness and use to cover the 28cm (11in) cake in the same way.

4 Roll out some more white sugarpaste to a 3mm (⅛in) thickness. Using the 2cm (¾in) round cutter, cut out 48 circles. Allow them to firm up slightly before using to create the polka-dot pattern on the blue cake. Secure each dot with a little water brushed onto the back.

5 Set the two covered cakes and board to one side and allow to dry out and firm up for a couple of hours.

6 Secure the larger cake to the centre of the covered board using a little buttercream or royal icing.

7 Take a length of greaseproof (wax) paper the same size as the circumference of the largest cake. Fold exactly in half, then into quarters, into eighths and finally into sixteenths. Unfold and place the piece around the outside of the cake. Use a pin to prick the sugarpaste through the paper in each fold position. This splits the cake evenly into sixteenths and marks exactly where the stripes should go.

TIP
Leaving the cut-out circles in position on your work surface for a couple of minutes will allow them to harden slightly so that when you lift them into position they shouldn't pull out of shape.

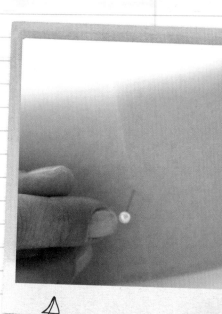

8 Roll out the deep pink sugarpaste into a long thin rectangle approximately 2–3mm (¹⁄₁₆–⅛in) thick. Using the pizza cutter create 2cm (¾in) wide strips. Trim the strips to 13cm (5in) long each. You will need 16 strips in total but it is wise to work with just four at a time, otherwise the sugarpaste dries out too quickly and your strips will crack.

9 Using the fluted pastry roller, mark stitching lines along the edges of the strips, approximately 3mm (⅛in) in from the edge.

10 Apply a scant stripe of water up the side of the cake and onto the top in the positions marked by the pinpricks. Secure each strip in place. Continue working around the cake until you have completed the striping.

11 To create the strip of ribbon around the base of the cake you will need two long strips measuring 40 x 3cm (15¾ x 1⅛in). Carefully lift them, supporting each strip with both hands to prevent it from ripping, and position in place. Each strip should go halfway around the cake. Trim the strips neatly at the back of the cake.

"Press lightly with the fluted pastry roller – it is only to indent the pattern, if you're not careful it will cut through the sugarpaste and you'll have to start all over again."

12 For the bow, make a strip approximately 14 x 3cm (5½ x 1⅛in) and mark the edges as before. Flip the strip over so the right side is facing the work surface. Fold each end of the strip in to the centre to create the bow. Lay a small strip over the centre of the bow and secure the ends behind. Apply a dab of water to the back of the bow and secure in position over the join in the strips at the front of the cake.

13 Dowel the base cake (see Stacking a tiered cake) and then lift the blue-and-white polka-dot cake into position on top, securing with a little buttercream or royal icing.

14 Using the 5cm (2in) cutter, cut out seven deep pink circles and cut each in half. Apply a little water to the back of each semi-circle and position around the base of the smaller cake.

TIP
Make sure the flat edge of the semi-circles sits down onto the base cake to cover any gaps between the two tiers.

15 Roll 14 balls of white sugarpaste around 1cm (⅜in) in diameter and position between each of the semi-circles. A dab of water on the base will hold them in position.

16 Trim the edge of the cake board with the white ribbon, securing at the back with a pearl-headed pin.

Butterfly cascade

PIPING A DELICATE DESIGN

A beautiful cake you really won't want to cut into. Slow the pace down and relax into creating this beautifully decorated cake.

Get it together...

- 30.5cm (12in) square cake, prepared for covering
- 35.5cm (14in) square cake board
- 30.5cm (12in) square cake card
- Sugarpaste: white
- Edible lustre dust: blue, pink and holographic sparkle
- Royal icing
- Piping (pastry) bags and no. 2 and no. 3 nozzles (tips)
- 12mm (½in) wide ribbon: pink and turquoise
- Pearl-headed pins
- Basic equipment (see Equipment)

1 Roll out the white sugarpaste to a 3mm (⅛in) thickness and cover the cake board (see Covering a board with sugarpaste). Set aside.

2 Place the cake on the cake card. Roll out some more white sugarpaste to a thickness of 5mm (³⁄₁₆in) and use to cover the cake. Trim any excess neatly and polish with an icing smoother (see Covering a cake with sugarpaste). Allow the board and cake to dry out overnight before assembling and decorating.

3 Apply a smear of royal icing to the centre of the covered cake board. Lift and position the cake squarely in the centre of the board.

4 Trace the butterfly template onto a piece of greaseproof (wax) paper (see Templates). Transfer the butterfly design onto the top of the cake, tracing the outline gently using the end of a paintbrush. The butterflies are clustered around the bottom right-hand corner and become more spaced out the further up the cake they go.

TIP
Setting the cake on a cake card to cover it makes the job a lot easier, the cake can then be transferred to the covered board the following day when the sugarpaste has hardened.

"Take great care when transferring a large covered cake as the sugarpaste is more liable to crack than with a small cake — make sure you support it underneath with your hands while moving it."

5 Take a little of each colour lustre dust and place each into a small bowl, with a soft paintbrush for each colour. Begin by dusting with the blue lustre dust to almost fill in each of the wings starting from the centre. Build up the colour from the centre of the butterfly each time to create the graduation.

6 Add in the pink highlights again from the centre of the butterfly but this time only one-third of the way into each wing.

7 Once you are happy with the colouring, dust over the entire wing of each butterfly with the holographic sparkle dust.

8 Fill a piping (pastry) bag fitted with a no. 2 nozzle (tip) with white royal icing. Play around with the consistency until you're happy with it – it should be liquid enough to pipe easily but firm enough that a piped line doesn't spread or break.

9 Slowly pipe around the outline of each butterfly wing in turn. Start in the top left-hand corner of the cake and work downwards and across so that you don't have to reach over the piped butterflies and risk smudging them. Pipe antennae and bulbs of royal icing down the centre of each butterfly (see Piping).

> **TIP**
> Tap the majority of the lustre dust off the paintbrush against the side of the bowl before putting it onto the cake, and build up the colour gradually.

> *"If you're not confident with piping, instead of working directly on your cake cut butterflies out of white sugarpaste. Once they have dried, colour the butterflies as described and pipe around their outlines. Allow to dry fully before transferring to the cake then continue decorating as described."*

10 Using royal icing in a piping (pastry) bag with a no. 3 nozzle, pipe straight lines around the top of the cake to form a frame. Over the straight lines, pipe a wavy line (see Piping).

11 Empty the royal icing from the bag into a small bowl. Add a couple of drops of water to loosen the consistency. Dip the end of a paintbrush into the icing and dot onto the cake to create the white dots.

12 Add a little of the pink lustre dust to the loosened icing and repeat the dotting method applying pink dots to each of the butterfly wings as shown in the photo.

13 Trim around the base of the cake with pink ribbon and the edge of the board with turquoise ribbon, securing at the back with pearl-headed pins.

Dotty dreams

CREATING A HIGH-IMPACT DESIGN

Let a round cutter do the design work for you! Combined with contrasting colours and a wired cake topper, this makes a stunning statement cake.

Get it together...

- Round cakes: 20cm (8in) and 25cm (10in), both prepared for covering
- 30cm (12in) round cake board
- Round cake cards: 20cm (8in) and 25cm (10in)
- Four plastic cake dowels
- Sugarpaste: white, turquoise and bright pink
- Buttercream or royal icing
- Round cutters: medium and small
- Posy pick
- 13 silver florists' wires
- 12mm (½in) wide pink ribbon
- Pearl-headed pins
- Basic equipment (see Equipment)

1 Roll out the turquoise sugarpaste to a 3mm (⅛in) thickness and cover the cake board (see Covering a board with sugarpaste). Set aside.

2 Place each cake on the corresponding size cake card and cover each with a thin layer of white sugarpaste (see Covering a cake with sugarpaste). Try to make this first layer as neat as possible – it will be covered up but will help get a super finish on your final layer. Allow the boards and cakes to dry out overnight before assembling and decorating.

3 Take each cake in turn, spray with a light mist of water and cover with turquoise sugarpaste rolled out to a 5mm (³⁄₁₆in) thickness, polishing to a super finish with an icing smoother.

4 Apply a small smear of buttercream or royal icing to the centre of the covered cake board. Position the 25cm (10in) cake in the centre of the board.

5 Dowel the base cake (see Stacking a tiered cake) and then lift the smaller cake into position, securing with a little buttercream or royal icing.

6 Take the medium round cutter and cut out circles from the turquoise layer. The drier white layer underneath will help when cutting out the circles, as you will feel when the cutter reaches it. Turn the cutter in a drilling motion around and around until the circle is cut out.

"To make the whole cake quicker – omit the balls around the base of each cake and trim with more of the pink ribbon instead."

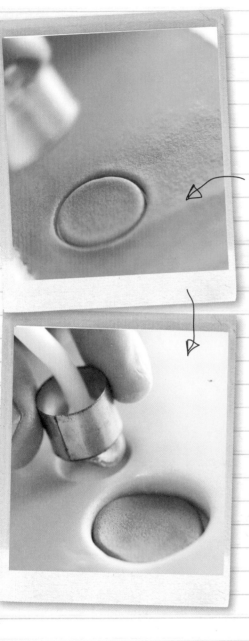

7 Cut out circles around the entire cake then repeat with the smaller round cutter.

8 Roll out some bright pink sugarpaste to around 3mm (⅛in) thick on your work surface lightly dusted with icing (confectioners') sugar to stop it sticking.

9 Using the cutters that made the holes, cut out bright pink circles, brush the backs with a little water and fit them into the cut-out holes. Repeat until all the holes have been filled.

TIP
The circles should come out with the cutter as you remove it. If they don't, help ease them out with a cocktail stick (toothpick).

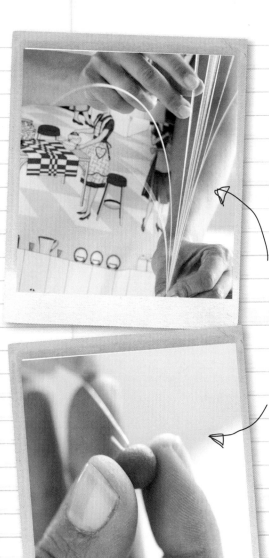

10 Roll a multitude of turquoise and bright pink balls and position in alternating colours around the base of each cake, securing with dabs of water.

11 To make the wired cake topper, take 12 lengths of florists' wire. Tightly wind the 13th piece of wire around the bases of the wires to secure them together (see Making a wired cake topper).

12 Push the wires into a small posy pick so that they sit tightly. Stand the pick in a potato or an apple to hold it steady while you work on it. Bend the wires into position by running them through your fingers – in the same way as you would curl a ribbon using scissors – and twist a small hook in the end of each wire.

13 Roll numerous small and medium balls of pink and turquoise sugarpaste. Insert the hooked end of the wires into the balls and squeeze lightly to secure. Add a ring of small balls in alternating colours around the base of the posy pick.

14 Trim the edge of the board with the pink ribbon, securing at the back with a pearl-headed pin.

TIP

If your wires don't sit securely inside the posy pick, place a small piece of sugarpaste in the base of the pick first.

"To roll out balls all the same size in double-quick time, roll out the sugarpaste evenly then use a small cutter to cut out equal sized pieces and roll into balls in the palm of your hand. For super smooth balls, grease your hands slightly with white vegetable fat (shortening)."

Troubleshooting

Cake decorating can be frustrating at times when things don't quite work out the way you wanted. I did this to a cake in my early decorating days, late at night and in sheer frustration (yes, my husband was rather alarmed!). Please try not to resort to this! Remember you're always learning, keep practising, appreciate what you have achieved and most importantly give it a go!

Get ready

• It is important to prepare a large cake properly for decorating, adding the buttercream/frosting layer which will stick the sugarpaste (rolled fondant) to the cake. Buttercream really needs to be made with butter rather than a margarine/low-fat spread so that when chilled it will set firm – that will not happen with spreads. This layer needs to be chilled until firm before covering your cake otherwise the filling in the middle of the cake will be soft and will cause an unsightly bulge in the sugarpaste around the sides of the cake.

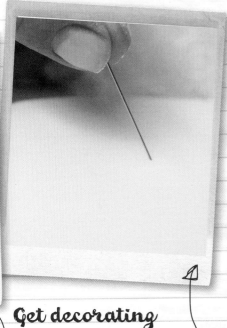

Get baking

• If your cupcakes suffer from a huge volcano effect when baked in the oven this has been caused by either too much mixture in the paper liners or an oven that is too hot. Try turning down the oven temperature next time you bake for gentler baking conditions for your cupcakes, allowing the centres of the cakes to cook at the same rate as the crust forms on the tops. Trim off the excess domes of your cupcakes before decorating if necessary – these trimmings are the baker's treat!

• I'm often asked what causes paper liners to peel away from cakes. There are a few things that contribute to this – the main culprit is moisture. Excess moisture can come from a range of places; lemon cupcakes are the worst for this, but underbaked cupcakes and using a margarine/spread with a

high water content instead of butter will cause it too. Make sure cupcakes are not allowed to cool in the tin (pan) too long before placing on a wire cooling rack. They will start to sweat and the steam will start to separate the cases from the cakes.

• Dry and burnt cakes can often be rescued by trimming away any burnt bits and then brushing them with a sugar syrup. To make the syrup, combine 180g (6½oz) caster (superfine) sugar with 225ml (8fl oz) water in a medium saucepan. Heat gently, stirring occasionally until the sugar has dissolved. Remove from the heat and allow to cool. You can also flavour this syrup with 5ml (1 tsp) vanilla, lemon or orange extract for an extra hit of flavour. This syrup can be brushed over the tops of cakes and will work to restore moisture. Useful in a baking emergency!

Get decorating

• Sometimes when rolling out sugarpaste, air bubbles can form within the paste and can ruin your beautiful finish. If this happens take a clean pin and pierce the centre of the air bubble and smooth the air out through the pinhole. Finish rolling out as before.

• Sugarpaste is a sticky substance to deal with and will try and stick to your work surface at any given opportunity. Keep checking the sugarpaste is loose and free from the surface when rolling out – keeping the surface lightly dusted with icing (confectioners') sugar. To stop it from sticking to your rolling pin, dust your hand lightly with the icing (confectioners') sugar and run the rolling pin through your hands. This should stop the paste from sticking without transferring white marks to the surface of your sugarpaste.

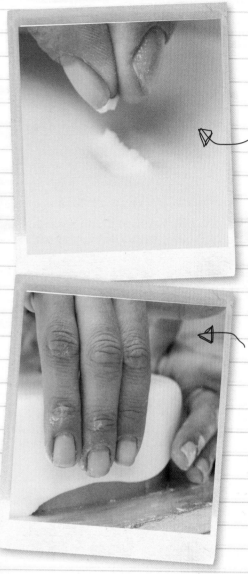

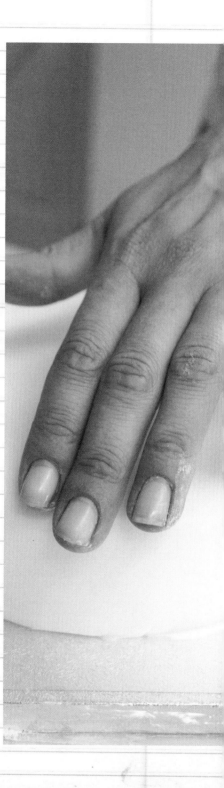

• Occasionally little bits will dive into white sugarpaste when you're rolling it out – if you spot them before the sugarpaste is the right thickness you can pinch them out lightly with your fingertips to remove them. Carry on rolling out to the correct thickness, which will smooth out the pinch mark leaving your sugarpaste blemish free.

• When covering a cake with sugarpaste, sometimes it is easy to misjudge when flipping it into place, leaving it slightly short of reaching all the way down one of the sides. If this happens, place your fingertips on the sugarpaste just above where the shortfall is. Move your fingertips in a circular rubbing motion, which will encourage the sugarpaste downwards to meet the base of the cake. You can cover up to a 2cm (¾in) gap with this handy technique!

• Cracks can often form around the top edge of a cake. To prevent this from happening, make sure to dust your surface lightly with icing (confectioners') sugar when rolling out, as too much will quickly dry out your sugarpaste and encourage the cracking. Roll out just enough to cover the cake without a large overhang of excess – too much and the extra weight will cause the sides to pull, again creating cracks. Small cracks can be sealed back together by rubbing gently with your fingertips in a circular motion.

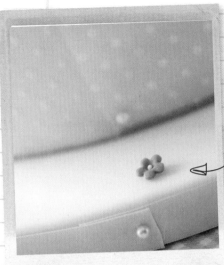

• If you have cracks or marks in your sugarpaste once you have covered your cake, it is always good to remember that there's always the back of a cake! Choose the best side to present as the front. Work design elements into your cake to disguise any small cracks, nicks or marks – a little blossom will do the trick!

• If there's a big gap in your sugarpaste (either at the base of a cake or elsewhere) that is quite large, roll out a little more to the same depth and cut out a piece to patch in. Rubbing the joins with your fingertips in a gentle circular motion will begin to blend them in. It's not a quick task, so keep massaging the sugarpaste and finish by smoothing with an icing smoother until it's as good as new and the joins are not visible.

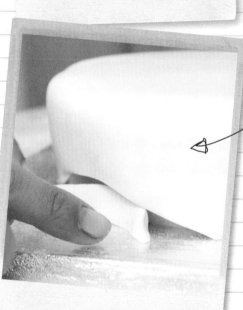

• If you end up with a large gap at the base of your cake when you have cut away the excess sugarpaste, consider using a wide ribbon to trim round the cake, which will disguise the gap.

• Getting the consistency of royal icing just right is always a bit of a battle, but time spent perfecting it before using it is definitely worthwhile. If it's too thick, add a couple of drops of water to loosen it slightly, and if too thin, then you will need to beat in more icing (confectioners') sugar.

• When piping lines or dots with royal icing, if you find there is a little peak at the finish point dab it down with a slightly damp paintbrush.

• When you're not happy with the positioning and finish of your sugarpaste when covering a cake and feel like admitting defeat, as long as you haven't smoothed it down and trimmed the excess, you can peel off the sugarpaste and start again. The used sugarpaste will have to be discarded, as it will be sticky with buttercream, but you can re-smooth your frosting layer, chill the cake again and roll out some new sugarpaste to cover the cake.

> "If something is going wrong and getting you in a tizz, take a deep breath, put the kettle on and have a cup of tea before carrying on! Taking a breather gives you the time to think about how to put things right."

Glossary

Buttercream/frosting – used to secure sugarpaste (rolled fondant) icing to cupcakes and to prepare a cake for covering with sugarpaste.

Cake board – also referred to as cake drums, 12mm (½in) thick. A solid non-edible base for cakes. Can be used covered with sugarpaste to complement your theme, or uncovered.

Cake card – thin foil-covered card used to mount cakes on for support when moving or when creating tiered cakes.

Cutters – cutters come in all sorts of shapes and sizes from the regular round and fluted cutters to decorative shapes such as blossoms and butterflies. Used for creating cookie shapes and for sugarpaste decorations, cutters can also have plunger ejectors often used with very small shapes, which release cut out shapes easily for you.

Double-sided tape – used to secure ribbon around the edges of cake boards.

Dowels – plastic or wooden rods, used to provide support within tiered cakes.

Dragees – sugar shapes, (e.g. balls and hearts) used for decoration adding a touch of sparkle, can be found in many many colours and sizes.

Edible glue – ready-made edible glue can be used in place of water. It is much stronger and a good investment if you'll be decorating regularly.

Edible lustre dusts and glitters – as the name suggests these are edible non-toxic powders and glitters that you can get in every colour under the sun. A great way to add a touch of glitz to a cake.

Embossing – imprinting sugarpaste gently with cutters or other items such as buttons to create a subtle pattern.

Florists' wire – available in white, silver, gold and a range of colours. Thicknesses vary from #20 (thickest) to #28 (thinnest). A medium-gauge wire (#24) is ideal for most tasks. Used to create wired cake toppers or stems for sugarcraft flowers. Available to buy from florists and cake-decorating suppliers.

Gel paste colours – used to colour sugarpaste and royal icing. They are extremely intense colouring and you will only need to use a small amount. These colours do not greatly alter the consistency of icing in the same way liquid colours will.

Greaseproof (wax) paper – a non-stick baking parchment paper used to line tins (pans). Also used for transferring templates onto cakes.

Icing smoother – a flat smooth plastic tool, similar to a paddle and used to polish covered cakes and boards providing a super smooth, glossy finish.

Icing (confectioners') sugar – used to prevent sugarpaste from sticking to work surfaces and as an ingredient in royal icing and buttercream.

Marzipan – an almond paste used with fruit cakes. A marzipan layer is applied to a fruit cake first before covering with sugarpaste. This seals in moisture and stops the fruit from staining through onto the sugarpaste layer.

Non-stick mat – using one of these to roll out your sugarpaste on will greatly cut down the need for dusting with icing (confectioners') sugar (and will help when it comes to clearing up too!).

Nozzles – also known as tips. They come in a variety of sizes and are used in conjunction with a piping (pastry) bag to pipe royal icing or buttercream. You may like to buy a basic set (I frequently use small round nozzles 1, 2 and 3) and then add more to your collection as needed. Look for seam-free ones for faultless piping.

Paintbrushes – Soft brushes, flat or round, are extremely useful for a number of tasks in cake decorating. Natural hair bristles are preferable to synthetic ones.

Palette knife – the ideal tool for covering cakes with a layer of buttercream before applying sugarpaste.

Pastry brush – silicone brush used for applying apricot glaze to fruit cakes.

Pearl-headed pins – used decoratively to disguise the join in a ribbon around a cake or cake board. The pearl heads also make the pins more easily identifiable for removing when serving.

Piping (pastry) bag – disposable or reusable bags which, when fitted with a piping nozzle (tip) and filled with icing, can be used to pipe decorations and borders.

Posy pick – a small pointed tube that sits within a cake to hold wires of a cake topper. Food safe, these prevent the wires from coming into contact with the cake.

Ribbon – used for trimming the base of cakes and around the edge of cake boards.

Rolling pin – a long dedicated sugarpaste rolling pin is the best item to work with for cake decorating. It is super smooth and non-stick and will give you the best results.

Royal icing – a thick icing strengthened with egg white. Royal icing sets firm keeping your chosen decoration in place. It is used to pipe lines and dots onto cakes for decorative detail, and also to pipe shell borders or snail trails around the base of a cake instead of using a ribbon.

Spray mister – small water sprayer ideal for spritzing cake boards before covering.

Sugarpaste (rolled fondant) – a smooth icing that can be rolled out and used to cover cakes. It can also be used to make decorations such as cut outs and models. It can be coloured to any shade desired.

Tin (pan) – used for baking cakes in.

Wired cake topper – a collection of wires and decoration that sprays from the top of a cake, giving a grand look.

Templates

Download a printable PDF of these templates
at http://bakeme.com/page/templates

Spring has Sprung

Butterfly Cascade

Suppliers

The Pink Whisk Shop
www.rucraft.co.uk/thepinkwhisk
Tel: 0844 880 5852
All the cake-decorating and baking equipment to get you started – and lots more besides! All products are chosen by me especially for you.

FMM Sugarcraft
Unit 5, Kings Park Industrial Estate,
Primrose Hill, Kings Langley
Hertfordshire WD4 8ST
Tel: 01923 268699
www.fmmsugarcraft.com
Sugarcraft manufacturers and suppliers of cake-decorating equipment

Kenwood Ltd
New Lane, Havant
Hampshire PO9 2NH
Tel: 02392 476000
www.kenwoodworld.com/uk
Kitchen electricals

Knightsbridge PME Ltd
Chadwell Heath Lane, Romford
Essex RN6 4NP
Tel: 020 8590 5959
www.cakedecoration.co.uk
UK distributor of Wilton products

Lakeland
Alexandra Buildings
Windermere, LA23 1BQ
Tel: 01539 488100
www.lakelandlimited.com
Bakeware and general kitchenware

Squire's Kitchen
Squires House, 3 Waverley Lane, Farnham
Surrey GU9 8BB
Tel: 01252 711 749
www.squires-shop.com
Creative products and services for baking and cake decoration

US

Global Sugar Art
625 Route 3, Unit 3
Plattsburgh NY 12901
Tel: 518-561-3039
www.globalsugarart.com
Icing and cake-decorating supplies

Pfeil and Holing
58-15 Northern Blvd
Woodside NY 11377
Tel: 800-247-7955
www.cakedeco.com
Baking and sugarcraft supplies

Williams-Sonoma
Locations across the US
Tel: 877-812-6235
www.williams-sonoma.com
Bakeware, kitchenware and kitchen electricals

Wilton Industries, Inc.
2240 West 75th Street
Woodridge 1L 60517
Tel: 630-963-1818
www.wilton.com
Innovative selection of baking and cake-decorating supplies

Australia

Baking Pleasures
PO BOX 22
Corinda 4075 QLD
http://bakingpleasures.com.au
Baking and cake-decorating products, tools and equipment

Cake Decorating Solutions
Shop B2 69 Holbeche Road
Arndell Park NSW 2148
Tel: 02 9676 2032
311 Penshurst Street
Willoughby NSW 2068
Tel: 02 9417 5666
www.cakedecoratingsolutions.com.au
Extensive collection of cake-decorating supplies

Iced Affair
53 Church Street
Camperdown NSW 2050
Tel: 02 9519 3679
www.icedaffair.com.au
Cake-decorating equipment and products

About the Author

Ruth Clemens writes the very popular baking blog The Pink Whisk. She is completely self-taught both in baking and cake decorating, by making cakes for friends and family. A passionate baker and decorator, Ruth's success just serves to prove that practice makes perfect! A contestant and finalist on the very first series of the BBC's *Great British Bake Off*, she also took part in *The Great British Wedding Cake* for the BBC, creating a stunning three-tiered traditional wedding cake – fit for a royal wedding, baked and decorated all within 12 hours – the ultimate busy girl's challenge! To keep up to date with Ruth's current ventures, please join the gang at facebook.com/ThePinkWhisk or on Twitter @thepinkwhisk
For more baking inspiration, recipes and tutorials visit www.thepinkwhisk.co.uk

Acknowledgments

My thanks go to a whole host of people who got this book off the ground and into print. My boys, Ashley, Dylan and Finlay, who have been patient through my projects, not eating things until they were given the go ahead and generally putting up with an extremely busy mum. My husband, Damian, who has taken over all the washing, cleaning, cooking (bacon and eggs counts as cooking doesn't it?) while I've been doing 'important' stuff. He is never-endingly supportive and everything I could ever have wished for. My family and friends who have pulled together to mind children, lend a constructive eye and generally point me in the right direction when I've gone 'off track'. Not forgetting their hugs too. To the masses that are 'The Pink Whiskers', busy girls (and boys) who have stuck with me through thick and thin, lending their support when it was most needed. Thoroughly lovely people, I couldn't wish for a better team standing behind me. Thank you to Kenwood and Pyrex for providing their products for use on our photoshoots. And last but not least, to the team I have had the pleasure of working with at David & Charles – Ali, Katy, Pru, Lorna, James, Grace and Ame. They have kept me and the book on the straight and narrow, spotting the potential in the first place and offering me the opportunity to get my first book into print. Thank you all of you.

Index

ISBN-13: 978-1-4463-0164-7 paperback
ISBN-10: 1-4463-0164-8 paperback

ISBN-13: 978-1-4463-5577-0 e-pub
ISBN-10: 1-4463-5577-2 e-pub

ISBN-13: 978-1-4463-5576-3 PDF
ISBN-10: 1-4463-5576-4 PDF

10 9 8 7 6 5 4 3 2 1

Publisher Alison Myer
Acquisitions Editor Katy Denny
Editor James Brooks
Assistant Editor Grace Harvey
Project Editor Ame Verso
Creative Manager Prudence Rogers
Production Manager Kelly Smith
Photographer Lorna Yabsley

Paperback printed in China
by RR Donnelley for:
F&W Media International LTD,
Brunel House, Forde Close,
Newton Abbot, TQ12 4PU, UK

F+W Media publishes high
quality books on a wide range
of subjects. For more great book
ideas visit: www.rucraft.co.uk